GW01374295

ARMS AND ARMOUR OF THE SECOND WORLD WAR

Jonathan S. Ferguson

CONTENTS

INTRODUCTION 5
THE BRITISH INFANTRY SECTION 9
THE GERMAN *GRUPPE* 35
THE ASSAULT 51
TRAINING TO KILL 69
CONCLUSION 89
FURTHER READING 91

INTRODUCTION

Weapons have left memories. The monotonous, repetitive bursts of the Bren, the hysterical shriek of the MG42's furious rate of fire and the lethal chatter of the Stens and Schmeissers all contributed to the cacophony of battle. Tracer bullets seared themselves into the memory. Fired from a distance, their parabola approached almost lazily until suddenly, like a swarm of fiery demons, they accelerated directly past one's head with ear-splitting cracks.
– Lieutenant Sydney Jary, Somerset Light Infantry

The Second World War was the single most important event of the 20th century. It established the strategic and tactical-level importance of aircraft and armoured vehicles with quick-firing artillery remaining king of the battlefield. Yet, as with all conflicts before and after, the war on the ground was fought by infantry engaging in countless firefights for which portable weapons were essential. The importance of this fundamental role can not be overstated. In a British training film of the period the filmed action was punctuated with the clear instruction, 'YOU MUST WIN THAT FIREFIGHT!' No battle could be won without successfully defeating – ideally, by killing – the enemy in most of these encounters. For the individual soldier, nothing could be more important to his well-being, survival, and ability to fight the enemy than his personal weapon and his only issued piece of body armour – his helmet.

In this sense, therefore, what we now call 'small arms and light weapons' were critical at this granular, small unit, *tactical* level of warfare. Thus many new weapons, ammunition types and pieces of equipment were developed by all sides, alongside new methods of fighting, in order to increase the chances of winning each firefight. Revised systems of training and manufacturing proved key to the eventual Allied victory. Each nation involved in the war determined its own idea of the best approach and philosophy toward winning. None were inherently better or worse, but certain trends were more forward-thinking than others and can still be seen in modern warfare.

Inspired by the Royal Armouries' exhibition 'Firefight: Second World War', this book charts the differing approaches taken to modernise small arms, associated training, and industrial infrastructure from the 1930s to the end of the war in 1945. It takes a British perspective but covers several theatres of war, placing into their tactical context the most iconic firearms of the conflict. Why were so many different types in use? Who used them, and for what purpose? And what, in an increasingly conflicted age, was their legacy?

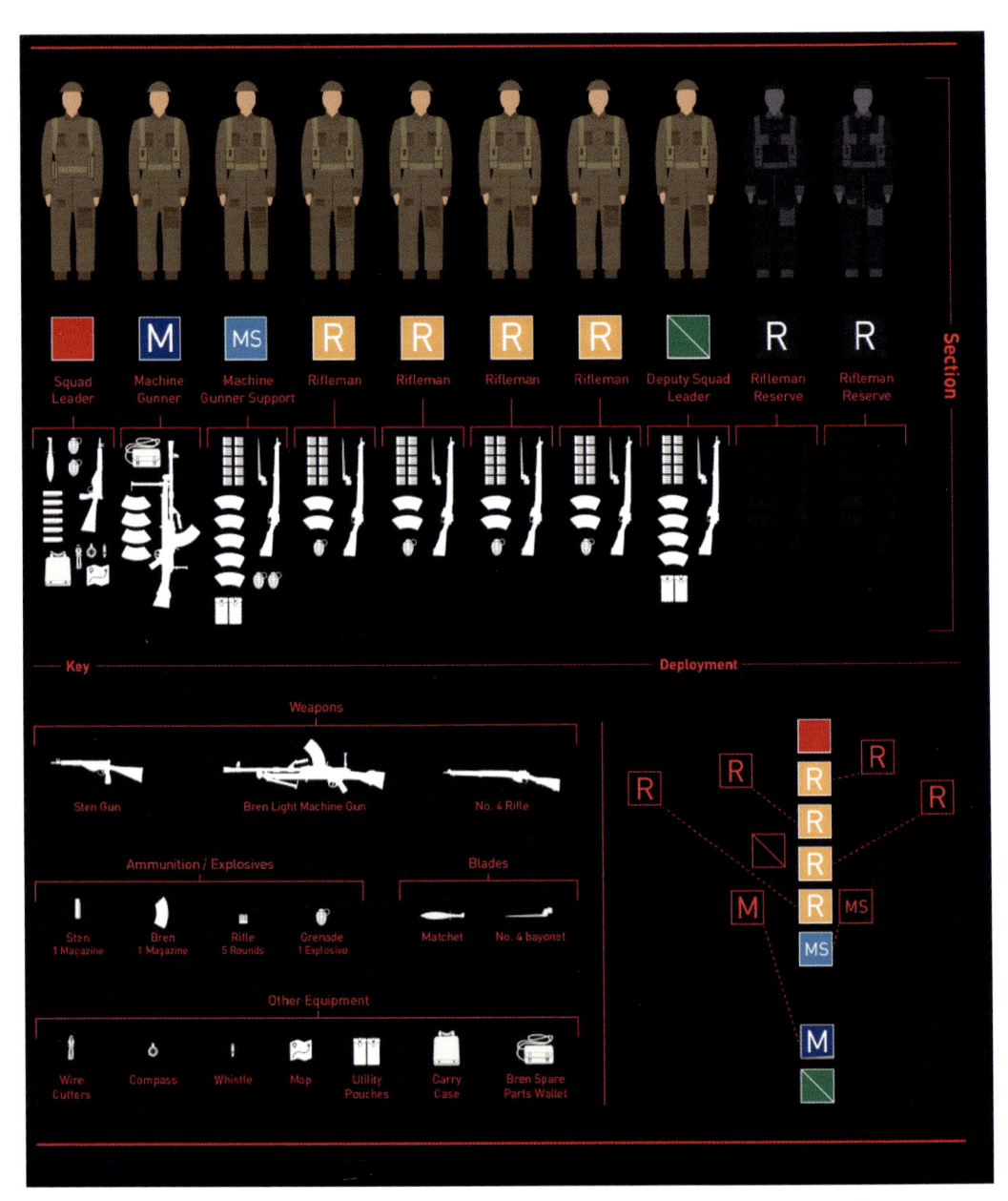

▲ Comparative dispositions of the British infantry section (this page) and German *gruppe* (facing page).

6 ARMS AND ARMOUR OF THE SECOND WORLD WAR

Zug

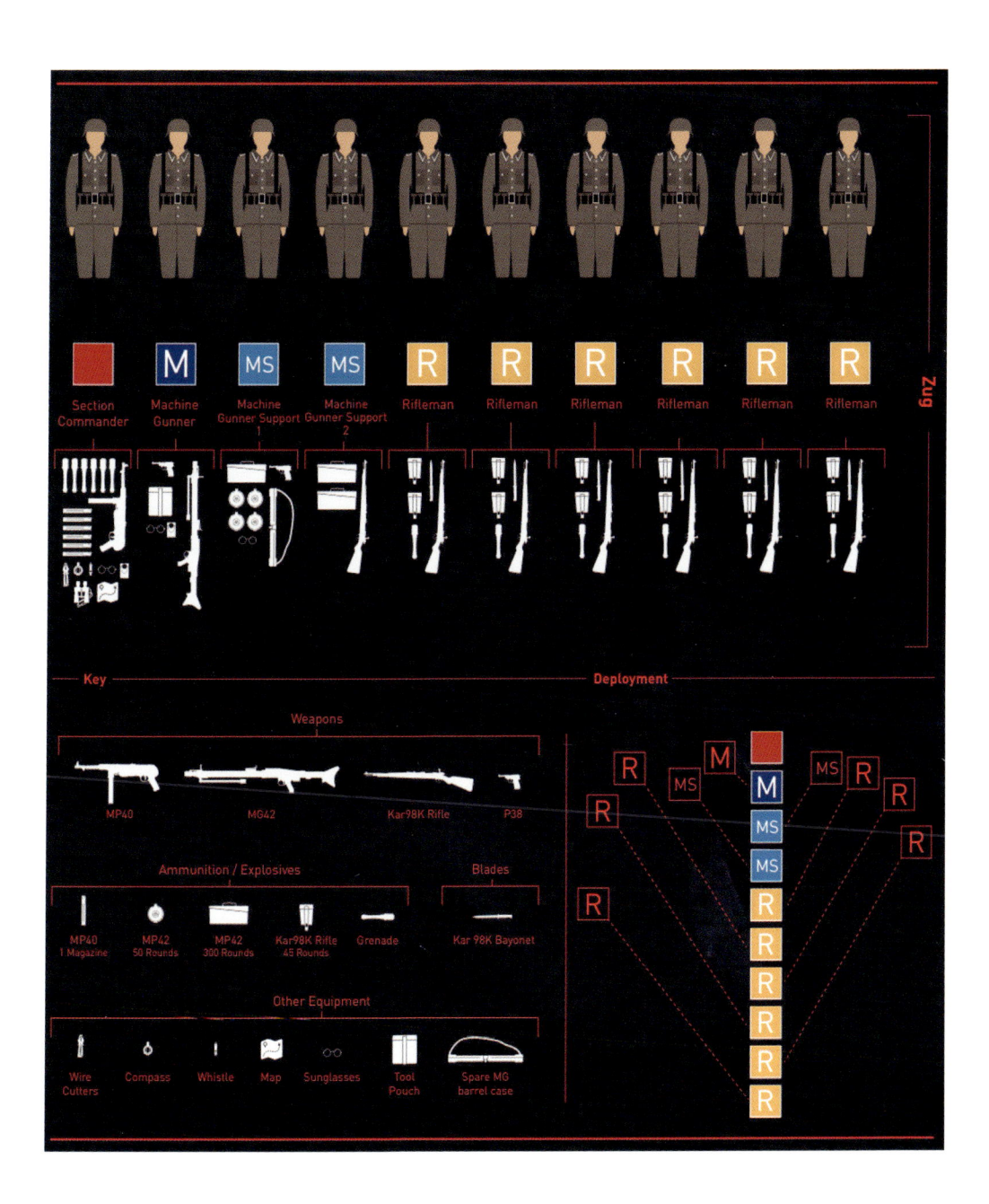

| Section Commander | Machine Gunner | Machine Gunner Support 1 | Machine Gunner Support 2 | Rifleman | Rifleman | Rifleman | Rifleman | Rifleman | Rifleman |

Key

Weapons
- MP40
- MG42
- Kar98K Rifle
- P38

Ammunition / Explosives
- MP40 1 Magazine
- MP42 50 Rounds
- MP42 300 Rounds
- Kar98K Rifle 45 Rounds
- Grenade

Blades
- Kar 98K Bayonet

Other Equipment
- Wire Cutters
- Compass
- Whistle
- Map
- Sunglasses
- Tool Pouch
- Spare MG barrel case

Deployment

▲ A British soldier ready to embark for France, 1940. His SMLE rifle and Pattern 1908 equipment will be replaced on campaign with the No.4 rifle and Pattern 1937 webbing. From *Picture Post*, 14 June 1940.

THE BRITISH INFANTRY SECTION

The purpose of infantry is to take ground from the enemy by force and hold it. Second War World armies mustered millions of men, but the building-block of victory was the smallest tactical unit on the battlefield – the squad. In the armies of Britain and its empire the squad was known as the 'section' and was led by a corporal. As then-Private Stanley Whitehouse, The Black Watch (Royal Highland Regiment) noted in his memoir *Fear is the Foe*:

It was the section that mattered to the private soldier. It was his military family; those seven or eight other men were his constant companions ... and he got to know them better, perhaps, than anyone in his whole life.

Although company-level support weapons – and indeed artillery, armoured vehicles and air power – could make a difference, the squad contained the minimum necessary people, arms, personal armour and ammunition to gain fire superiority.

Following this 'building block' logic, two to four squads (depending upon the nation and date in question) constituted a platoon, which was, in turn, the smallest tactically *effective* infantry unit and the smallest led by a commissioned officer. It allowed each squad to be equipped and resupplied as appropriate for the tactical situation and included a pool of additional arms not routinely carried at squad level (typically mortars and anti-tank weapons).

In most depictions of Second World War combat in war movies and video games, there is little rhyme or reason to how each soldier is armed and no clear picture of how weapons, roles and tactics interrelate. Main characters (and/or character classes within video games), such as snipers, might be given distinctive weapons directly relevant to an assigned role, but typically arms are generic or assigned based upon the personal preference or personality of the character. In reality, every individual soldier in a squad was assigned an appropriate weapon for their specific role in that fight (even if the battlefield reality often departed from the textbooks). As such the equipment of the squad changed over the duration of the conflict as new items were issued and tactical lessons were learned.

For Britain, at least, the number of men remained constant at eight men with an additional one or two kept in reserve. The section was sub-divided

▲ King George VI firing the Bren gun, lynchpin of the British Section, RSAF Enfield, 1940.

into a rifle group of four riflemen led by the section commander, and a Bren gun group comprising No. 1 and No. 2 gunners led by a lance-corporal who was second-in-command. Only the No. 1 Bren gunner stowed his personal rifle with the platoon's baggage, thus the first wartime incarnation of the infantry section relied entirely upon the Bren for automatic fire. Every other weapon was a bolt-action rifle, for a total of seven. However, every man in the section carried ammunition for the Bren, underlining its importance as the 'base of fire' for the whole section (see p. 13) or as author and soldier George MacDonald Fraser put it, 'the section's most precious possession'. Even the additional 50-round bandolier of ammunition that was permitted as an option was allocated for refilling Bren magazines. In 1941 the Thompson and (increasingly) the Sten replaced the section commander's rifle and he carried five or six magazines. In 1944 his two magazines for the Bren were removed, perhaps reflecting the importance of his role as lead assaulter.

As with other nations the most common broad tactic was for the two groups to 'leapfrog' each other in order to provide mutual fire support on the advance (or if falling back). The same was true at platoon level with, typically, three sections (numbered No. 1, No. 2 etc) working together with the support of the platoon's two-inch mortar (attached to the platoon headquarters which would usually also be controlling the battle) delivering either high explosive rounds or smoke to conceal the advance. In a platoon attack one section would normally suppress as another advanced, whilst another (usually No. 2 section) would work its way to the rear to cut the enemy off from either retreat or reinforcement. Alternatively the section Bren groups and platoon support weapons (PIAT, mortar, snipers, Vickers etc) could be brought together to create overwhelming fire, allowing a group of riflemen to press the enemy (with others bringing up Bren ammunition). A platoon might group together its sections for an assault, by grouping all three Brens and platoon weapons together in support and using the most experienced riflemen as an assault group. In one instance in Normandy, 36 Bren guns, an entire battalion's worth, were deployed together in anticipation of an attack that did not come.

Although not featured in this book, the ongoing and important role of the Mk.I Vickers-Maxim gun (introduced in 1912) is deserving of mention. Unlike the Lewis gun, no modern replacement for this belt-fed 'sustained fire' or 'heavy' machine gun was forthcoming. Although the Bren could be fitted to a tripod for longer range or defensive fire, its firepower was limited by its 30-round magazines and could not hope to equal the range or volume of fire offered by the Vickers. As a result, the venerable Vickers remained in service at platoon level throughout the Second World War and beyond. Only 11,828 new Vickers guns had to be made during the war for front-line service, thanks to 15,000 remaining in service and stores from the First World War. However, 64,183 barrels, 13,207 locks and 19,205 tripods were produced, to say nothing of the millions of .303 cartridges required to feed these guns. Although tactical emphasis was upon the Bren, the importance of the venerable Vickers in support and in defence cannot be underestimated. In addition, 7,071 Colt-made Vickers guns in the US .30-06 calibre were acquired under Lend-Lease and equipped the Home Guard, who perhaps had the greatest need for sustained fire in static defence in the event of German invasion.

▲ A British section advancing through barbed wire. Somewhere in the Middle East or North Africa, c.1943. BEN 85

◀ A section of the Kings Own Yorkshire Light Infantry at Elst, Netherlands, 2 March 1945. The section equipment of Bren, Sten, No.4 rifles and P'37 webbing are all clearly visible, along with a PIAT launcher.
© IWM B 15008

The Bren gun was the most important British infantry weapon of the Second World War. Although it became an iconic British service weapon, it was designed by Czech firm Zbrojovka Brno with feedback from the Royal Small Arms Factory (RSAF) at Enfield (North London). The famous name combines the two locations, 'Brno' and 'Enfield'. The Bren was lighter and less bulky than the Lewis gun of the First World War and, after initial teething problems with fouling of its gas regulator, more reliable.

BREN .303 IN LIGHT MACHINE GUN

The Bren gun was the most important British infantry weapon of the Second World War. Although it became an iconic British service weapon, it was designed by Czech firm Zbrojovka Brno with feedback from the Royal Small Arms Factory (RSAF) at Enfield (North London). The famous name combines the two locations, 'Brno' and 'Enfield'. After initial teething problems with fouling of its gas regulator, it was more reliable and lighter than the Lewis gun of the First World War.

The Bren was not merely a like-for-like replacement for the Lewis but an evolution of the light machine gun concept. On its introduction in 1937 the British section was reorganised around it. It was a lightweight weapon with a 500-round-per-minute rate of fire, less than half that of the belt-fed German MG 42 (at 1200 rounds per minute). This combination limited firepower but allowed for maximum movement and flexibility in the attack. Its main role was to suppress the enemy with a slow but steady rate of fire to allow the rifle group to close with and/or outflank them, and to fix them in place until the assault could be pressed home. Everyone in the Section was trained to use the Bren, meaning that the gun would keep firing if the gunner was injured or killed.

The riflemen also carried magazines for the Bren and although their rifles also fired .303 ammunition, most of what they carried was preloaded into Bren magazines that they were expected to pass to the Bren gunner as needed (the rest being carried in charger clips for their own rifles). The Bren gunner had an assistant ('No. 2 Bren') who was in effect another rifleman but assisted in various ways as needed. He could quickly take up the gun if the No. 1 was incapacitated, and assist in reloading when employing 'rapid' fire. In the defensive role he would again support in reloading, coordinating ammunition supplies, and changing the barrels to prevent overheating. Defensive fire could be given from the integral bipod, by resting the folded bipod to allow rapid target acquisition or, in static defence where there was time to set the gun up, on traditional machine gun 'fixed lines' of fire on a dedicated tripod mount. The tripod doubled as an anti-aircraft mount when fitted with either an additional leg or, in a clever piece of design, an ordinary SMLE rifle by means of the rifle's bayonet lug. Brens were even set up on the south coast of England in anticipation of invasion, despite the far greater sustained and defensive fire potential of the Vickers.

British reliance upon the Bren was critical to modernisation efforts. However, this caused particular problems following the emergency evacuation of British forces from Dunkirk in mid-1940, since 27,000 of the total 30,000 Brens produced to date had to be abandoned in France.

Despite the training and equipment of the section favouring the Bren, and its capability as a highly mobile light machine gun, the rifle group was theoretically the main manoeuvre and assault element as it had been in the First World War. The Bren may have been regarded as the key firearm, but its role (in theory at least) was specifically that of fire support. Period training pamphlets and films specify that the section commander lead with his submachine gun ready at the hip. The Bren group followed, but with the weapon carried at the slope. Once in action, military doctrine dictated that it be kept concealed for as long as possible, both visually and audibly, by firing single shots until either the 'slow' (30 rounds per minute) or 'rapid' (120 rounds per minute) rates were deemed necessary.

▶ The Bren Light Machine Gun, Mk.I. The first Bren gun ever made, produced in 1937. PR.6982

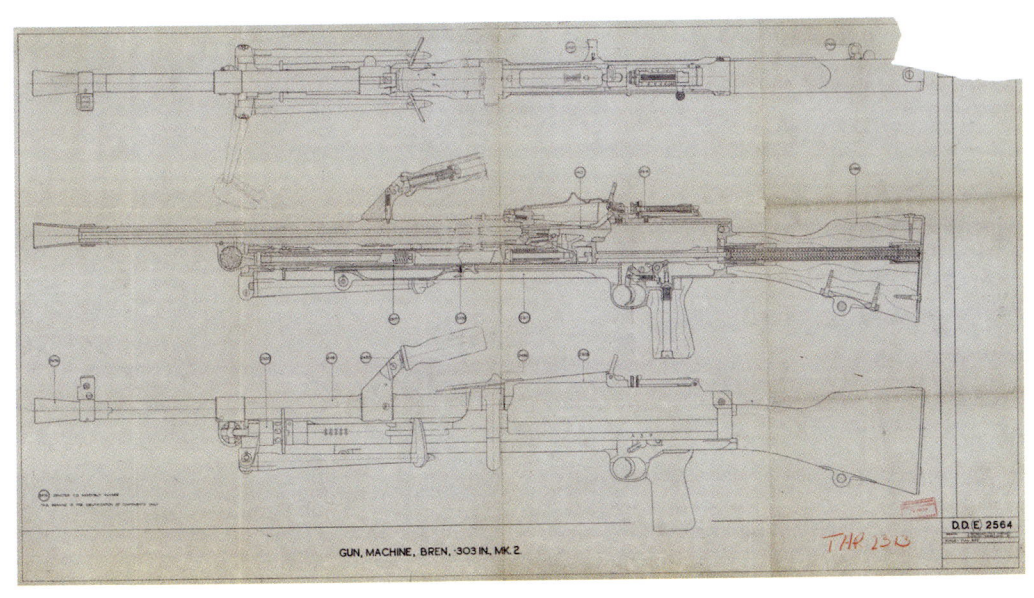

▲ RSAF Design Drawing for the Mk.2 Bren gun, August 1944. © Crown Copyright

Having delivered its fire support, the Bren group was then supposed to redeploy to the rear of the position as the rest of the section made the final assault. There they would eliminate any stragglers and take up a fire support position. This despite the greater accuracy of the Bren, which would favour it continuing to attack the enemy position, and its greater mobility, which made it well-suited to being fired from the hip in the assault. In reality, the Bren gunner did often lead the section or join the assault or even spearhead it. Bill Cheall recalled an ambush in which three soldiers were killed by a burst of 'Spandau' fire. His platoon commander ordered an ad hoc 'strong patrol' to flank the enemy machine gun post and it was the Bren gunner who killed the two Germans.

Bren was also often fired from the hip in the assault, especially if more than one section attacked at once, or if a section was able to obtain a second Bren. Bill Cheall, a Private in the 6th Green Howards, recalled one instance: 'We all jumped up, firing our weapons, as we had all lost pals and were as mad as hell. Our Bren gunner, a tough kid, was really on the boil and ran forward firing the Bren from the hip, with his Number Two changing magazines as they ran.'

This was especially true in urban and jungle fighting, and in emergencies where the firepower of the Bren was urgently required. One such case from Italy in 1945 involved Royal Marine Commando Corporal Thomas Peck Hunter. Although exceptional, this incident epitomises the relative merits of the Bren's mobility and the devastating firepower of the MG42. According to his Victoria Cross citation he:

THE BRITISH INFANTRY SECTION 15

... seized the Bren gun and charged alone across two hundred yards of open ground. Three Spandaus from the houses, and at least six from the North bank of the canal opened fire and at the same time the enemy mortars started to fire at the Troop.

Corporal Hunter attracted most of the fire, and so determined was his charge and his firing from the hip that the enemy in the houses became demoralised. Showing complete disregard for the intense enemy fire, he ran through the houses, changing magazines as he ran, and alone cleared the houses. Six Germans surrendered to him and the remainder fled across a footbridge onto the North bank of the canal.

The Troop dashing up behind Corporal Hunter now became the target for all the Spandaus on the North of the canal. Again, offering himself as a target, he lay in full view of the enemy on a heap of rubble and fired at the concrete pillboxes on the other side. He again drew most of the fire, but by now the greater part of the Troop had made for the safety of the houses. During this period he shouted encouragement to the remainder, and called only for more Bren magazines with which he could engage the Spandaus. Firing with great accuracy up to the last, Corporal Hunter was finally hit in the head by a burst of Spandau fire and killed instantly.

There can be no doubt that Corporal Hunter offered himself as a target in order to save his Troop, and only the speed of his movement prevented him being hit earlier.

◀ Corporal Thomas Peck Hunter.
© John Swinny

▲ Part of a Section of British Commandos pictured during a raid in occupied Norway in 1941. The Section Bren is clearly discernible in silhouette. BEN 177

The use of the Bren as a sort of ersatz assault rifle was so prevalent that by the time of the post-war Malaya conflict Brens were carried by 'point men' on combat patrol, equipped with front pistol grips and tracer ammunition to allow fire to be 'walked' onto enemy targets. This formalised the use of the Bren in a 'machine carbine' role, after the period British term for a submachine gun.

Regardless of its potency as an automatic weapon, doctrinal emphasis upon accurate single shots, the inherent mechanical accuracy of the gun and its excellent recoil buffering all contributed to the Bren's reputation for accuracy. Famously, some thought it *too* precise for a machine gun. There is some truth to the myth that the Bren was indeed relatively accurate for a machine gun of the era. It is, approximately, as accurate as the modern L7 General Purpose Machine Gun (GPMG) that ultimately replaced it, an impressive feat for a 1930s design. Far from being a hindrance, this was a tactical advantage, making for more efficient use of ammunition while still being effective in both killing the enemy and suppressing them. Although not a sniper rifle, the Bren *was* used to hunt snipers using both single shot and bursts, being as accurate as many of the rifles then used for actual sniping. Had the planned No. 32 telescopic sight been adopted, it would have been even more effective in this role. The same scope was later chosen for the No. 4 (T) sniper rifle. The redundant dovetail mount for the scope

▶ The Bren Mk.I deployed on its bipod. PR.6982

remained on the Bren in the Mk. I variant. It could even be used in what would now be described as the 'Sharpshooter' or 'Designated Marksman Rifle' role, its low recoil and effective bipod allowing for relatively accurate and rapid single shots out to several hundred yards. This level of skill was uncommon, however. In his book *To Salamaua* (2010) Philip Bradley quotes Private Norm Bear of the 2/3 Independent Company, Australian Army as he recollects the actions of Private George 'Les' Poulson in engaging Japanese soldiers trying to set up a machine gun:

He killed seven of them before they woke up to the fact that they shouldn't be trying to do it. Sniping with a bloody Bren gun, single shot, bloody incredible.

Another Bren gunner, Eddie Head, was able to shoot no less than eight Germans in the head in a single engagement.

Some sections appropriated a second Bren, as did Stanley Whitehouse's section in the Reichswald Forest (1945). This provided for two mutually-supporting fireteams with near-equal firepower. Nor did actual issue at section level always reflect doctrine. Bill Cheall noted:

[They] arrived in France in 1940 poorly equipped. Each company only had two Bren guns and one Boys – and nobody had yet fired these weapons in training. No mortars, not even revolvers for officers. All they had was rifles (Cheall was a territorial called up in August 1939. Battalion was technically a labour battalion upon initial transfer to France).

Cheall also spoke of the love that his section's Bren gunner and assistant gunner had developed for their all-important weapon:

… taking turns to carry it and despite all the mud and filth we had gone through, it was spotlessly clean. Those two grand lads eventually brought it back to England and there was almost a court martial about it. All weapons brought back from Dunkirk were supposed to be handed in and then redistributed at a later date. However, the Bren gunner was adamant that the weapon should remain with his platoon. Eventually, a higher-ranking officer agreed with his sentiments and the lad was almost overcome with emotion.

Regardless of how it was used, the Bren was critical to the operation of the section in all phases of the firefight and in all theatres of operation, providing highly mobile fire support to the rifle group in British and Commonwealth service (other than in the British Indian Army, which pre-emptively adopted the Vickers-Berthier Mk III instead).

NO.4 MK.I .303 IN RIFLE

This variant of the long-lived Lee service rifle was first adopted in the 1930s but was not mass-produced until the loss of 330,000 SMLEs at Dunkirk. Produced in quantity from 1941 at Royal Ordnance Factory Maltby (South Yorkshire), ROF Fazakerley (Liverpool) and BSA Shirley (Warwickshire), it became the primary British infantry rifle by 1943.

However, many soldiers continued to use the same Short Magazine Lee-Enfield (now known as the 'Rifle, No. 1') that their fathers and grandfathers had carried. It was in fact still in production from 1940 to 1943 at the Birmingham Small Arms company's Small Heath factory (Birmingham), and the Royal Small Arms Factory at Enfield manufactured many parts so that damaged or worn out rifles could be kept in service throughout the war. Those in the Middle East and North African theatres retained it throughout the war, as did Commonwealth troops.

▲ No.4 Mk.I .303 calibre rifle. PR.10338

▲ Cutaway. PR.5899

THE BRITISH INFANTRY SECTION 21

The intent of the redesign was primarily to take advantage of modern machining methods and thus reduce time and cost of manufacture. This is evident in the square shape of the receiver (the steel body into which the barrel, bolt and magazine are fitted, a 'body' in British parlance). This also made the weapon more robust. In practical terms, little changed with this new Enfield. The No. 4 fired the same .303 cartridge as before and handled very similarly to the SMLE, loading in exactly the same way via five-round charger clips. Troops would have had little difficulty in switching from one to the other, the primary difference for the user being sights. The SMLE's 'open' combat-style sights were mounted close together and could be aligned quickly for a 'snap' shot at a fleeting target – a lesson learned from the Boer War. The No.4 received a flip-up micrometer-adjustable rear sight mounted on the body of the rifle, increasing the sight 'radius' and signalling a philosophical shift back toward target-style accurate shooting at distance. It did however retain a simple Sten or Bren-style loop aperture, visible with the sight flipped down, for close-range fighting. A heavier profile barrel and new target pattern sights were fitted, theoretically improving accuracy (while retaining a simple loop rear aperture as a battle sight. Wartime pressures resulted in many rifles (like this one) being fitted with simplified rear sights (made from bent sheet metal or even simple two-position flip sights) and barrels featuring only two rifling grooves instead of the usual five. As the Allies began to turn the tide of war, the proper sights and barrel were again fitted to new rifles.

▼ The wartime expedient flip aperture-type rear sight of the No.4 rifle. The battlesight range of 300 yards is marked on the sight – the smaller aperture was for 600 yards. PR.10338

▲ No. 4 rifle fitted with bayonet. PR.5899

Another change was to abandon the long and heavy Pattern 1907 sword bayonet in favour of a small, light, and cheap form of the 18th century socket bayonet. This reflected the bayonet's modern role as a mainly psychological tool, a device for controlling prisoners of war, or a weapon of last resort. The bayonet was no longer decisive in combat, but period training refused to recognise this, probably due to the need to foster the necessary aggression and willpower to win a firefight. In extreme situations it also allowed (as it always had) a soldier who was out of ammunition to have some hope of fighting and obtaining a better weapon. Soldier and journalist Tom Wintringham published several magazine articles and a book (*New Ways of War*) emphasising the dominance of modern military technology and the obsolescence of the bayonet. This view seems to have been borne out by actual experience. Sydney Jary reported having seen one of his men use a bayonet to kill a German on one occasion and that bayonets were typically used to open ration tins. Similar stories abound throughout the 20th century as actual use of the bayonet declined.

Bolt-action rifles in general were simple and usually reliable, and the No.1 and No.4 rifles were no exception. George MacDonald Fraser, who regarded the Enfield as 'the most beautiful firearm ever invented', commented that 'cased in wood from butt to muzzle, [it] could stand up to any rough treatment, and never jammed'. Complaints about the Enfield were rare, but like any firearm it did, in fact, jam. Stanley Whitehouse, fighting in winter conditions in the Ardennes, noted:

… our personal weapons froze up and to cock a rifle we had to hammer the bolt in position with a piece of wood, a stone or any other handy object. We were issued with graphite grease to rub on the mechanism, but it too froze.

As noted previously, despite its slow, manually operated mechanism and limited 10-round capacity, it was the Enfield rifle and bayonet (along with grenades) that were expected to press home the assault phase of any section or platoon attack.

STEN MK.II 9 MM SUBMACHINE GUN (MACHINE CARBINE)

Much has been said about the poor quality and unreliability of the Sten gun, based in part upon post-war experiences with worn-out guns and American-made replicas not matching the original specification. This reputation is far from a recent concoction, however. Many veterans were at least sceptical, if not outright dismissive, and this has legitimised scorn for the type. George MacDonald Fraser called it the 'plumber's nightmare', a nickname that has stuck (more often in ironic form as 'plumber's delight').

Problems certainly emerged in the rush to tool up and churn out hundreds of thousands of guns. An automatic weapon is only as good as its springs, and depends upon the correct geometry of its magazine and magazine housing for proper feeding of rounds. The views of Sten critics are summarised by the recollections of Captain Dickie Davies of the Royal Norfolk Regiment (Kohima, 1944):

Four Japanese ran out of one of the bunkers. I pressed the trigger, and nothing bloody well happened – my Sten gun jammed. They always jammed, a useless weapon. I threw it at them – I was so annoyed.

The experience of veterans cannot be discounted, and defective magazines and guns doubtless found their way into the hands of troops as the balance between quick manufacture and quality control was sought. With no traditional safety catch, numerous accidental discharges occurred, eventually mitigated (if not solved) by adapting the cocking handle to serve as a bolt-lock.

▲ This Mk. II Sten Machine Carbine is shown fitted with the Mk. I Bayonet, rarely used in practice. XII.7202

▲ Component parts of a Sten gun being assembled at a Royal Ordnance Factory, July 1942.

▲ A cutaway Sten Mk.II showing the trigger mechanism. The cocking handle is locked into the safe position. PR.7353

However, from a strategic point of view the Sten was a major achievement and arguably a war-winning weapon. It provided every Section commander (as well as specialist troops like paratroopers) with the close-range rapid-fire weapon that they needed. Emergency procurement of Thompson guns could only be a stopgap and the Lanchester gun was deemed too time-consuming to mass-produce. Development of the STEN (named for designers Shepherd and Turpin and, most likely, the Enfield factory) began in 1940 and the Mk.I gun was ready for issue by mid-1941. This was further simplified to create the definitive Mk.II variant in late 1942. This served throughout the war, supplemented by the Mk.III (see p. 28–30) and, as the desperate need for guns subsided, the higher quality Mark V. Ultimately, 3,839,171 Sten guns of all marks were produced during the war and the type was extensively copied. The contradiction of the Sten as the essential yet undesirable weapon is summarised perfectly by Captain C. Shore of the Royal Air Force Regiment:

We wanted a killing weapon – at once; and we got it; but during its lifetime its killing propensities were not wholly confined to the enemy! No prima donna, ballerina or tennis star was ever more temperamental than the Sten gun.

PATTERN 1937 EQUIPMENT

This equipment carried everything a soldier would need in combat. Like the Pattern 1908 equipment of the previous war, it was made from cotton 'webbing' material that soldiers were supposed to constantly maintain with layers of 'Blanco' cleaning powder, giving a uniform green or khaki colour. The key difference lay in two large pouches at the front. These carried 120 rounds (in loaded magazines plus spare cartridges) for the unit's Bren light machine gun. This left only 50 dedicated rounds for the rifleman's own No. 4 rifle – 70 rounds fewer than in the First World War. This change resulted from the new focus upon the Bren and Sten guns as the main sources of section (squad) firepower. The rifle was regarded by the authorities as little more than a self-defence weapon, although the rifleman remained key to taking ground from the enemy. The soldier designated as 'No. 2' for the Bren

▲ The large ammunition pouches of the Pattern 1943 web equipment, designed around the Bren magazine. XIII.1193

▲ A section training together with the Bren No.1 and his No.2 nearest the camera, the supporting riflemen behind them. All are wearing Pattern '37 webbing with Bren ammunition pouches. © IWM H 000099

THE BRITISH INFANTRY SECTION 27

gun could carry a second set of Bren magazine pouches ('utility pouches') on his upper chest. This was a less comfortable arrangement than the standard pouches, as Alex Bowlby of the 2nd Battalion the Rifle Brigade recalled:

The only place to wear them is round your neck. They hung round mine like pendulums in a gale. The weight of the magazines – ten pounds – forced my chin onto my chest. As I walked they yanked at my neck. I cursed them aloud. They yanked back.

Other essential components included a bayonet hanger (or 'frog') and a haversack pack for kit such as additional clothing, knife and fork, and water bottle. The section commander also carried cutters to get through enemy barbed wire.

MARK III COMBAT HELMET

When Germany launched its lightning offensives in 1940, it caught the Allies off-guard. The British Army had expected this war to resemble the last, and was equipped with a helmet much like that used during the First World War. This Mk.II helmet focused on protection from above in anticipation of a return to trench warfare.

This began to change in 1941 when the Medical Research Council began work on a new design. Made of the same manganese steel, it was deeper with a more rounded 'skull' and flared brim, improving protection for the sides of the head. This was far more suited to the modern, mobile war in which fighting now primarily took place above ground. In this respect it was closer to the German *Stahlhelm*, although it was undeniably bulkier than that iconic design. It also sat square on the head, whereas the Mk.II was often worn at a rakish tilted angle, exposing one side of the head to injury. The intent behind retaining a bowl-shaped helmet was to keep costs down and speed up production.

The Mk.III was painted in olive green and often fitted with a scrim net for attaching camouflage. The overall shape gave rise to the popular nickname of 'turtle helmet'. The Mk.II liner and chinstrap were carried over, the liner being a suspension type comprising a piece of leather cut with five flaps laced together at the top, providing an adjustable internal 'cap' with a gap between the hard outer shell and the head. This limited the potential for injury via shock or deformation of the steel. It also allowed for circulation of air to keep the head cool and limit chafing. Unlike the *Stahlhelm* it had no

▲ The British Mk.III helmet showing its turtle shell-like form, intended to better protect the sides of the head. IV.1883

ventilation holes in the shell. Like all steel helmets of the conflict the Mk.III could, at most, stop a pistol bullet but this was not its primary purpose.

The Mk.III entered production in November 1943 but was not issued en masse until the following summer. It was produced by Briggs Motor Bodies Ltd. of Dagenham (Essex) and the Rubery Owen Company of Leeds. The first examples went to British and Canadian units for the D-Day landings in summer 1944. Though unable to fully replace the Mk.II during the war, the Mk.III became a more familiar sight with British forces as VE-Day drew nearer. The liner was modified in 1945 to be removable, permitting use as a water bowl and prompting a change in designation to Mk.IV. As a result only half a million Mk.IIIs were ever produced. The liner was altered again post-war to create the 'Mk.V' (an unofficial designation). However, the steel 'turtle' shell remained unchanged until the 1980s when the ballistic nylon Mk.6 was adopted.

The First World War had seen limited use of body armour due to the static nature of fighting on the Western Front, but a return to mobile warfare meant that no armour vests were issued to or even privately purchased by the infantry. This lack of physical protection was addressed by John Langdon-Davies in an August 1940 article for *Picture Post*. To augment the Mk.II helmet, Davies advised adoption of slitted steel goggles for the eyes and body armour that comprised steel plates with an additional repurposed entrenching tool blade over the upper chest. Davies directly references medieval armour in his article and, indeed, the added plate is clearly based upon the medieval gorget. However, in concept it also foreshadowed later solid steel or ceramic plates used in today's body armour. Modern soldiers also wear ballistic eye protection as suggested by Davies, albeit with transparent lenses. Unfortunately, sufficiently lightweight materials capable of stopping rifle calibre bullets had yet to be invented, and so soldiers continued to fight wearing only steel helmets.

▶ Proposed body armour for soldiers: *Picture Post*, 31 August 1940.

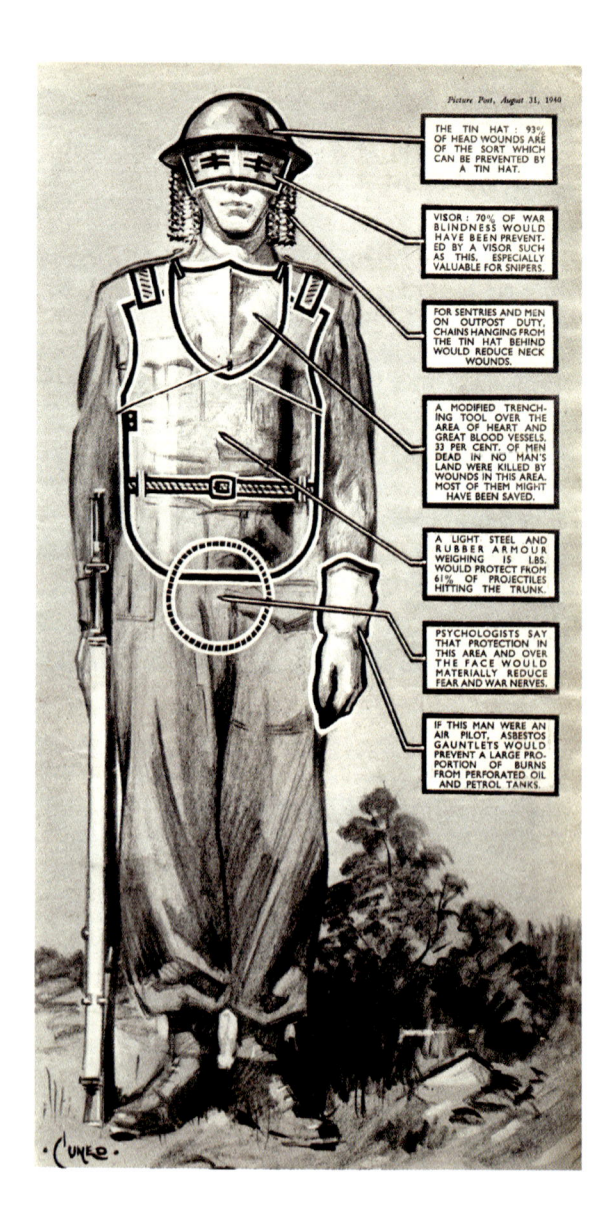

PROJECTOR, INFANTRY, ANTI-TANK (PIAT) MK.1 LAUNCHER

The oft-derided PIAT was introduced in late 1942. Like the Boys rifle that it largely replaced (see p. 82), the PIAT was not issued at section level by default but as needed from a pool of three launchers per company. Unique among wartime anti-tank weapons it was not a recoilless gun or rocket launcher but a shoulder-fired spigot mortar. The immense recoil of a heavy mortar bomb, normally planted into the ground for firing, was absorbed by means of an enormous spring (although contrary to myth, this did not propel the bomb). This had to be cocked manually for the first shot, which as Stanley Waterhouse noted, 'required a squaddie with the strength of Hercules' and in the face of the enemy would have to be operated while lying on one's back. The spigot was effectively a long and thick firing pin that provided support for the bomb at the moment of firing by which time it was fully inserted in the tail of the bomb. It then recoiled against the spring and was caught by the trigger mechanism ready for the next shot. If the shooter failed to provide sufficient resistance with his shoulder to the recoiling weapon the spigot would fail to travel far enough to re-cock and would have to be manually operated again.

With this tremendous recoil, and weighing in at a hefty 14.7 kg, the PIAT was inferior to German or US anti-tank weapons which could be fired from the shoulder. Nonetheless the PIAT was far better than any anti-tank rifle. Provided the target could be hit, it was capable of penetrating the armour of even the mighty Tiger tank. Indeed, although an exceptional feat, Major Robert Henry Cain VC was able to destroy or disable four Tigers (out of a total of six enemy tanks) during the Battle of Arnhem. This was possible because, like the German anti-tank weapons, the PIAT employed a shaped-charge warhead. This harnessed the 'Munroe effect', using high explosives to turn a cone of copper into a hyper-velocity jet of particles that could cut through 100 mm (3 in) of steel armour.

Despite its intended role, the PIAT was also used against other vehicles, structures and even against enemy soldiers in the open. Stanley Whitehouse in *Fear is the Foe* describes a night attack by German troops in the Netherlands, October 1944. His section's Bren had suffered a stoppage, so he improvised with the PIAT:

▲ The PIAT bomb with its distinctive elongated fuze-holder, intended to provide the necessary 'stand-off' for the shaped-charge jet to form. Three bombs could be carried in a special container for ready use. PR.1551

THE BRITISH INFANTRY SECTION

▼ The PIAT complete with canvas sling, cheek-pad, and butt-pad. PR.1551

My heart gave a flutter as I saw a German helmet, then another and a third against a sliver of silver skyline … "Enemy front!" I bawled. "Enemy front!" Pointing the PIAT towards the silhouettes I fired. A mighty explosion erupted down the lane, followed by weird shouts and screams.

Seven German soldiers were killed by the blast of the bomb, with another four succumbing to high-velocity fragments from the casing. Thanks to its mortar heritage the PIAT was also given an official secondary role as a light mortar, firing indirectly in a pronounced arc. Alex Bowlby, who regarded it as 'an effective but alarming' anti-tank weapon, felt that it was a much better infantry mortar than the actual platoon 2-inch mortar.

NO. 36M MK.1 'MILLS BOMB' GRENADE

The Mills bomb could be thrown up to 35 yards (32 metres). This was not as far theoretically as the German stick grenade, but it was much more compact for carrying. It was virtually identical to the original 1915 No.5 design, modified in 1918 to accept a screw-on 'gas check' disk for use with the SMLE rifle cup discharger. The 'M' variant was modified with shellac resin for waterproofing purposes and became the standard-issue grenade during the Second World War. Its cast-iron casing shattered into sharp, high-velocity fragments. Its deep grooves were designed to result in consistently sized square pieces and although this did not prove to be the case the grooves were retained as they reduced weight and gave good grip for handling.

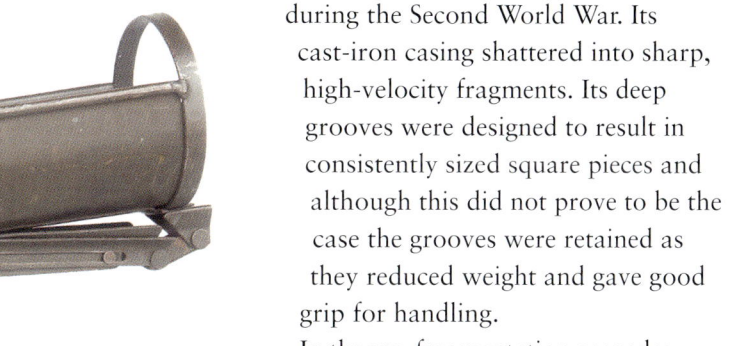

In theory, fragmentation grenades were intended to be used in a defensive role, with 'blast' grenades used to stun defenders as an assault went in. This also reduced the risk of accidentally wounding a comrade. In reality, the First World War had already shown that 'frag' grenades were far more effective in the assault, and consequently all combatant nations relegated 'blast' grenades to a training role by 1939 (although the blast grenade later returned in the form of the 'flashbang'). One aspect of First World War practice that took longer to change was the allocation of hand grenades to designated 'bombers' within the rifle group who each carried two fragmentation and two smoke grenades. From 1944 the 'bomber' role was abolished and a greater complement of ten grenades distributed more evenly throughout the section (although an emphasis on the rifle group was still retained): two for the section commander, one each for the four riflemen, and two for the Bren No.2. At the same time the section's complement of ammunition was reduced (by around 14% for the rifle) and Bren (12%).

Grenades were essential in attacking trenches and machine-gun posts as well as hardened structures like bunkers and pillboxes. Although firearms could be shot into viewports or entrances, well-designed structures were more resistant and provided arcs of fire that made it difficult to get close enough. Even earth and sand offered significant protection against small-arms fire, and required either launched or thrown explosives to indirectly attack the occupants. Kenneth Cooper of the Border Regiment writes of reinforced Japanese dugouts:

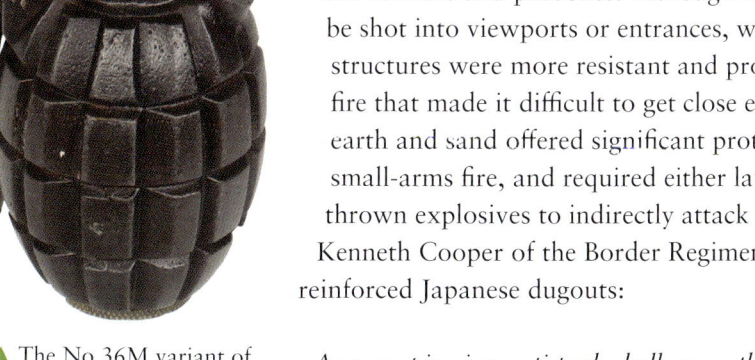

▲ The No.36M variant of the First World War-vintage Mills grenade. XX.4924

Armour-piercing anti-tank shells were the only missiles which could really inflict damage on them. Infantry on

THE BRITISH INFANTRY SECTION 33

their own had somehow to penetrate close enough to lob phosphorous bombs or Mills grenades through the loopholes.

Sydney Jary describes the use of the hand grenade against an MG 42 machine gun post in occupied France:

A long burst of Spandau fire reverberated through the wall immediately opposite where I now crouched. I pulled the pin from my grenade, let the lever fly off and, after counting three, tossed it over the orchard wall. There was the usual "crump!" I remembered so well from grenade ranges, and a clatter of feet as one or two people ran back up the lane towards Vernonnet. Later, at the rear of the town, we found their shattered bodies. They had bled to death from the awful wounds inflicted by the jagged pieces of 36 Grenade.

As Jary's account shows, even if blast or fragmentation did not prove instantly lethal, it would, within its blast radius of perhaps ten metres, almost certainly either incapacitate or prompt swift retreat or surrender. Although the Mills remained standard issue, several specialist grenades were in use, such as the No. 77 smoke grenade which infantry could use to create their own cover and was also used for clearing bunkers via its deadly white phosphorous content.

▲ This image from a British training manual shows the correct way to throw a hand grenade.

34 ARMS AND ARMOUR OF THE SECOND WORLD WAR

THE GERMAN *GRUPPE*

The German equivalent of the British section or US 'squad' was the *gruppe* or group. Like the UK, Germany had modernised its squad on the basis of a new machine gun – the MG34. It represented a leap forward in machine-gun technology, far lighter and more mobile than the old Maxim pattern guns but still fed by a long linked belt of rifle ammunition. The jacket of cooling water was replaced with a perforated steel heat-shield and (like the Bren) a replaceable barrel to prevent heating from affecting accuracy and barrel life. More importantly however, it was conceived as a 'universal' or 'general purpose' machine gun. Whereas the Bren could fulfil a basic defensive role (for which it had to be specially equipped), a GPMG must be capable (like a Maxim pattern gun) of sustained defensive or long-range fire but also be capable (like the Bren) of being quickly and repeatedly repositioned in the attack. This demanded a dedicated training programme and specialist machine gunners, unlike a light machine gun that could be integrated into ordinary infantry training. The adoption of a rapid fire and belt-fed gun reflected German emphasis (with machine guns) on volume of fire over precision, both for effective defence and withering suppressive fire in the assault.

Although the organisation and equipment of the *gruppe* differed from the Section, tactically they were not so different. Initially the *gruppe* comprised distinct machine-gun and rifle teams but by 1943 German doctrine had the entire *gruppe* act as one unit, more like the Section in that respect. However, the demands of operating a belt-fed gun still required a three-man crew – gunner, assistant gunner and ammunition carrier (who typically remained to the rear with his rifle until resupply was needed). The MG34 and MG42 were true crew-served weapons whereas despite a theoretical two-man crew for the Bren it could be operated by the gunner alone. Regardless, both nations treated the machine gun and its gunners as the primary weapon in a firefight.

The German gun in particular was found 'front and centre' in any given formation. It acted as the spearhead of the assault, firing and manoeuvring onto the enemy position as the riflemen provided deliberate aimed fire in support of it. Ironically, given its greater weight, bulk, and appetite for ammunition, German doctrine dictated that the machine gun would not hang back or relocate while the riflemen assaulted the position. It was to continue to deliver fire unless the risk to friendly soldiers was too great, in which case the gunner would assault while firing from the hip. Then, just as in the British case, the brunt of the assault was borne by (as the US manual 'German Squad in the Attack' puts it, translated from the German) the 'vigorous shock power of the riflemen with bayonet' and by hand grenades.

MG42 7.92 MM MACHINE GUN (*MASCHINENGEWEHR*)

The MG34 saw service throughout the war, and in modified 34/41 form was capable of a rate of fire up to around 1,200 rounds per minute. In fact it is likely that many Allied accounts referencing 'Spandaus' refer to MG34 variants. The gun that captured the military and popular imagination was the improved MG42, with its even faster rate of 1,300-1,500 rounds per minute. Like the Bren and indeed Vickers, both MG34 and MG42 were supplied with a mount for static defence. Similar to earlier mounts, the 'Lafette' stabilised the gun sufficiently to allow fire out to 3,200 metres but also included an advanced mechanism for laying the gun. This could be set up to automatically shift the gun to create smaller or larger 'cones' of fire at a given distance. Like the Bren mount it could also be converted to the anti-aircraft role, something to which the German guns were theoretically better suited. In reality, engaging 1940s high-performance aircraft from the ground was rarely successful.

▲ A 1945-dated MG42 installed on the Lafette mount, used for defensive or long-range fire. PR.13317, PR.80

British troops were often apprehensive of engaging troops equipped with the MG42. Stanley Whitehouse referred to it as 'the dreaded Spandau' and wrote of its 'chilling, unmistakable sound'. 'Spandau' was a nickname for any German machine gun derived from the factory where many were made; Maxim MG08s had been referred to as 'Spandaus' in the First World War. In a description from the fighting in the French countryside in 1944, Whitehouse highlights the psychological, as well as the potentially lethal, effect of the weapon in Bocage country: 'a Spandau opened up with its unmistakable purr – like cloth being torn – and our lead section was chopped down – 2 dead, 3 wounded and the other 2 seemed all right – just too terrified to move'.

▲ British soldiers inspecting captured MG34s both on the bipod and static mount. Libya, c.1943.

One MG42 was able to keep an entire British company at bay for some time, although this was less to do with its rate of fire and more due to the firing of judiciously short bursts, which prevented the British from locating and tackling it. It took two three-inch mortar barrages to silence it. In other words, whereas the gun was highly effective and psychologically affecting (even without long bursts of fire), it could have been any well-manned machine gun causing similar problems. Sydney Jary also

▲ The machine gun team of a German *gruppe*. Russia, 1943 or 1944. © Bundesarchiv

references the suppressive effect of MG42 fire at Elst (part of Operation Market Garden):

It was the most devastating display of small arms firepower that I experienced throughout the campaign. Long bursts of Spandau fire tore through the Company positions. Branches and slithers of wood from the fruit trees flew in all directions and furrows were torn in the earth, sending grass and soil flying into the air. The parados [rear] of our slit trenches failed to stop this concentrated fire and showers of stones and soil were thrown onto my soldiers crouching below.

The effectiveness of the MG42 and/or its gunners sometimes led soldiers to compare the MG42 negatively with their own Bren. Recalling a particularly intense firefight Alex Bowlby remarked that 'compared with the Spandaus they sounded like pop-guns'. Jary implies that the claimed superiority of the Bren was down to War Office propaganda and took a view on the manning of the MG42 that appears at odds with the German doctrine of a separate machine gun group and proactive team of riflemen:

Like most infantry subalterns trained in the UK for the invasion of Europe, I was convinced of the excellence of our Bren light machine gun. After 40 years, I still view the Bren with affection. It was excellent, particularly as a highly portable and accurate infantry section weapon invaluable in the attack. However, when it came to a fire fight between a German and a British platoon, their MG34 and MG42 won hands down. I remember my first reaction to actual infantry warfare in July 1944 was one of amazement at the crushing fire power of these very rapid-firing guns. It seemed to me that the German infantryman seldom used his rifle. He was a carrier of boxes of light machine gun ammunition of which they seemed to have an endless supply.

It is safe to say that the MG42 was a technically good design and that the psychological effect of the gun was not merely (as US propaganda painted it) 'all bark, no bite'. The gun was psychologically effective *because* of its technical capability and the training of its crews, and all of this made for a tangible firepower advantage, especially in the defence. A well-manned and commanded MG42 group could, quite simply, keep more heads down than its British equivalent. All else being equal, a British section or platoon would have to fight harder or longer, utilise some other 'force-multiplier', or exploit the accuracy and mobility of the Bren to overcome the inherent firepower disadvantage. The tactical lessons learned were clear: the vast majority of post-War armies issued a belt-fed machine gun at squad level even if they augmented it with a more mobile light machine gun. Nonetheless, in the right situation, short bursts from a judiciously manoeuvred Bren might be as effective as 50 rounds from a less mobile MG42. Properly utilised within the system of fighting laid down for them, the guns *could* be (effectively) evenly matched. Thus the MG42 was not the wonder-weapon that it is sometimes painted as, nor was it inferior *per se* to the Bren. Bowlby's own view changed over the course of the war and reflects this nuanced reality:

I had always had the idea that because of its rate of fire – eleven hundred rounds a minute [sic] compared to the Bren's six hundred – one Spandau was worth two Brens. Now I realised that such a tremendous rate of fire must make the gun difficult to control, and really accurate shooting impossible. As a scatter-gun, at night, at long range, or for continuous fire – here the Spandau, belt-fed, scored heavily over the Bren – the Spandau was supreme. But for accuracy it was the Bren every time.

Although Germany lost the war, its military technology was of great interest to the Allies and others. The MG42 was one of several highly influential weapons, influencing many armed forces to re-equip with general-purpose machine guns, including the MG42 series itself, which was adopted by Spain, Greece, the former Yugoslavia, and is still used by Iran and Pakistan. It also remained in service in West Germany and the current variant, the MG3, is only now (at the time of writing) still being phased out of Bundeswehr service.

MP40 9 MM SUBMACHINE GUN (*MASCHINENPISTOLE*)

Germany was far ahead of the UK in terms of submachine-gun development, having pioneered this class of weapon at the end of the First World War with the MP18 *Maschinenpistole*, followed by the MP28 and – just before the hostilities began – the completely new MP38. Anticipating its role as a paratrooper and vehicle crew weapon, it was lighter and more compact. It incorporated an under-folding stock for ease of storage and carriage (later copied for use on the Kalashnikov rifle) and omitted the wooden furniture and metal barrel shroud of previous designs to reduce weight. Development continued, however, replacing the machined receiver tube and magazine housing with sheet metal, making the revised MP40 better suited to a wartime economy. Whereas the British Army dictated (in theory) aimed single shots as the primary means of fire, the MP38/40 was geared toward automatic fire, lacking a semi-automatic setting and featuring heavy buffering to prevent the impact of the moving bolt on the rear of the receiver. The result was a more expensive gun than the Sten but a more reliable and controllable one despite a similar rate of fire (500–550 rounds per minute).

▲ An MP40 with folded stock and sling. PR.7365

THE GERMAN *GRUPPE* 41

As a PIAT gunner, Stanley Whitehouse's only issued firearm was an Enfield No.2 revolver with which, he claimed, 'you could barely hit the sea from a dinghy'. He chose to replace it with a captured MP40 which he credited with saving his life:

Training now took over. After firing at night move your position or hide. Being unable to move I ducked. It was not a second too soon. A long burst of the dreaded Spandau raked the front of our 'slitter', hurtling my small pack, pouches and pistol over my head and away into the night. Luckily the Schmeisser, its spare magazines and the grenade fell into the trench. The enemy were now roaring, as though making a charge, but were still invisible. I stuffed the spare magazines into my blouse, grabbed the Schmeisser and emptied it in their direction, spraying it from side to side … I stood up and hosed another magazine down the road, this time finding relief by shouting, 'Come on you bastards, come on'. I was becoming hysterical, but the shouting seemed to release a pressure valve and I clipped on another magazine – the last – and emptied it in the general direction of the enemy. 'Come on you Hitler bastards, come on', I yelled as I fired …

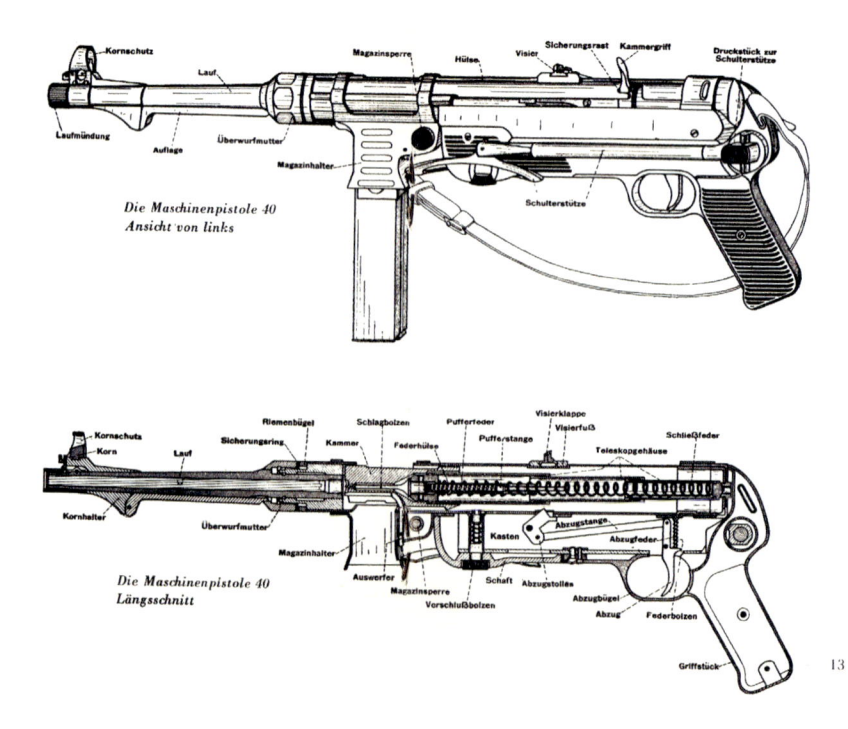

▲ From the training manual *Die Maschinenpistole 40 Beschreibung und Handhabung* (Heinz Denckler-Verlag, n.d.).

42 ARMS AND ARMOUR OF THE SECOND WORLD WAR

▲ This *gruppe* is headed by the squad leader with his MP40 (right). The assistant squad leader (armed with a rifle), the machine gun team, and the rifle team follow. France, 1944. © Bundesarchiv

MAUSER KAR98K (*KARABINER* MODELL 98 KURZ) 7.92 MM RIFLE

Like the UK, Germany retained its battle-proven bolt-action rifle, shortened and lightened in 1934 to better suit modern mobile warfare, and to standardise on one type of medium-length rifle rather than issuing separate short carbines for artillery and other units. Also like their British counterparts, most soldiers in the *gruppe* were armed with it and expected to use it throughout the attack. The Mauser had only a five-round magazine, but since rifle ammunition on both sides was loaded in five-round clips, this was in practice less of a disadvantage than it might appear. Several bayonet types were in use but the most common on the front lines was the Seitengewehr Model 1884/98, a short knife-type bayonet. Unlike the UK, however, Germany did successfully develop a self-loading rifle in the form of the Gew43, as well as the *Sturmgewehr* series, but were unable to produce enough to supplant the Kar98k. The Mauser served throughout the war and long beyond Germany's defeat in 1945 in both military and civilian hands.

▲ German soldiers with their Kar98k rifles. At their waists are leather pouches for ammunition clips. © Bundesarchiv

WALTHER P38 SELF-LOADING PISTOL

The *Pistole* 38 was adopted as the replacement for the iconic P08 Parabellum or 'Luger' pistol in 1938. Although benefitting from many years of development in firearms technology, it fired the same 9 mm cartridge and retained an eight-round capacity. It was chosen for its much simplified design, making it quicker and cheaper to make using modern machinery. Although designed by Walther, like many military firearms it was produced by several manufacturers including including Walther and Mauser. Mauser's own HSv pistol had been trialled against the Walther and failed, but Walther's production capacity was lacking. As a result, Mauser found themselves manufacturing their rival's design instead.

Although the intent had been to replace the Luger, the actual need for pistols in the German armed forces was so great that the Luger remained in production until 1944. The two pistols saw service together until war's end. Both were issued to officers, vehicle crews, and machine gun crews, among others. The P38 design survived post-war, seeing widespread service with West German military and police forces. It was replaced by the *Pistole* 1, which was simply the P38 of the Second World War era with a new name.

▶ 1943-dated examples of the P08 (right) and P38 (over page), produced and issued in parallel throughout the war. PR.4077, PR.4202

▶ The simplified P38 lent itself to more rapid production, something that is evident on this example with its obvious machining marks. In peacetime these would have been polished smooth. Nazi Germany developed several designs for an even simpler and cheaper *Volkspistole* ('People's Pistol') to arm the *Volkssturm* civilian militia, but these were never introduced and both P38 and P08 served until war's end.

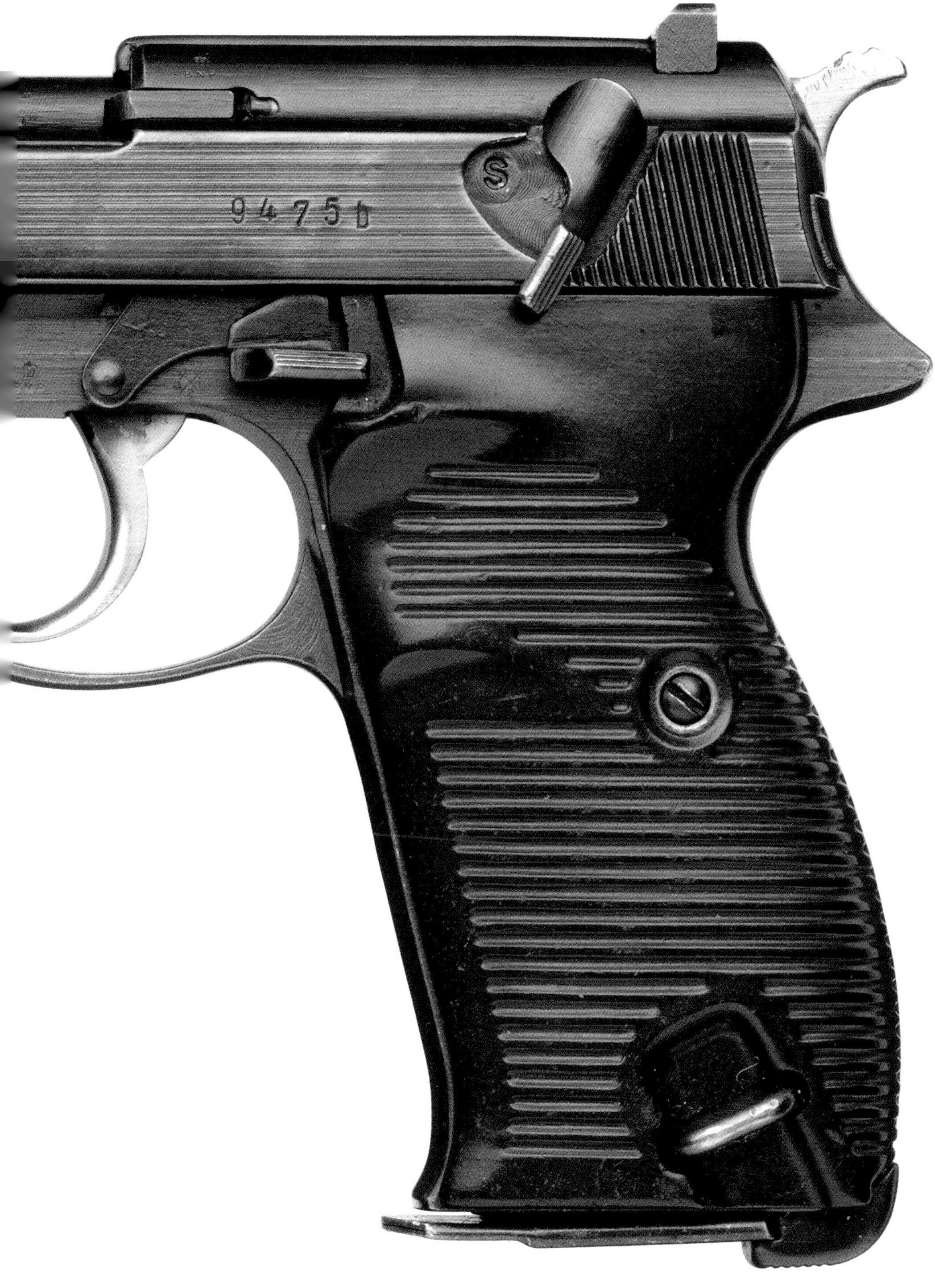

MODELL 1943 *STIELHANDGRANATE*

The German infantry entered the Second World War with the Modell 1924 stick grenade, in turn based upon the First World War original, and used this throughout the war. Following the wartime trend a simplified variant was introduced alongside it in 1943. This featured a solid wooden handle rather than the hollow earlier form, the igniter pull-cord now being accommodated in the nose of the grenade. The long handle of stick grenade allowed soldiers to throw it further than smaller Mills or 'egg'-type grenades (up to 40 metres). As issued the grenade was theoretically a blast grenade for offensive use, stunning the enemy but producing little fragmentation (reducing weight for increased distance and minimising the risk to the attacker from their own weapons). For defensive use, an additional sleeve

▲ A German rifle grenadier with Kar98K rifle fitted with 30-mm *Schiessbecher* ('shooting cup') grenade launcher and M43 *Stielhandgranate*. Netherlands, September 1944. © Bundesarchiv

was to be attached, adding significant fragmentation effect. For longer range, one soldier in the German *gruppe* was issued with a 30-mm *Schiessbecher* ('shooting cup') attachment for his rifle. Versions for attacking both enemy soldiers and armoured vehicles were created.

MODELL 1935 *STAHLHELM*

The basic German pattern for a steel helmet (*Stahlhelm*) was introduced in 1916 and was reminiscent of the 15th-century sallet design, with low sides and elongated rear to protect the neck, although it incorporated a pronounced brim at the front that was absent from the medieval original. The sallet had been designed to protect against edged and impact weapons as well as arrows. The modern equivalent was intended to shield the wearer from artillery shell, mortar bomb, and grenade fragments and was highly effective. It offered greater protection than the British Brodie which was itself analogous to a medieval design – the 'kettle hat'. Designed to be cheap to manufacture, it protected only from overhead threats. All of these of course had to protect against trench weapons like clubs.

The *Stahlhelm* was the best design of the war and became the symbol and name of the German veterans' organisation '*Der Stahlhelm*' in the interwar period. The new design debuted in 1933, the same year that Hitler came to power. It abandoned steel construction, instead being made from *Vulkanfiber* or vulcanised paper. The new design was far less bulky, fitting the head more closely and shortening the visor and sides, which also allowed for better hearing. It was, however, insufficiently protective for combat and was replaced by the M1935, made to the same basic design but returning to a steel alloy. Weight was similar to the First World War original at around 1.4 kg for the largest size. Around 2.5 million M1935s were produced by seven different manufacturers across Germany.

Unlike the 1916, 1917 and 1918 models, the M1935 was exported to and copied by several other countries, including Spain, Hungary and China. Revised patterns were introduced in the form of the M1940, with simplified ventilation-hole rivets, and the M1942 which allowed for manufacture from a single steel pressing, eliminating the internally rolled edge of the earlier forms and creating a square profile. All three variants were fitted with the Modell 1931 liner (introduced in 1934), comprising a leather suspension piece with eight ventilated flaps laced together at the top, with a felt band to prevent rubbing and fitted to an aluminium (later steel) supporting band. The band in turn was mounted to the shell with domed split pins. The chinstrap was a narrow leather type with adjustment buckle. These variants were closely based on the M1935 and all were worn throughout the war, although not all units were issued this basic pattern (notably paratroopers used a more compact design). The M1935 design also inspired many later helmets including, ironically, the replacement for the long-serving Second World War US M1 steel helmet, the PASGT. As a result, this was informally dubbed the 'Fritz' on its introduction in 1983. To this day Chile uses its stock of M1933 helmets for ceremonial purposes.

▲ This example of the M1935 *Stahlhelm* is painted for air force (*Luftwaffe*) troops. The Army (Heer) version was identical but painted dark green. IV.1831

◀ A Modell 1935 German *Stahlhelm* penetrated by a rifle bullet or high velocity shell fragment. Steel helmets of the era were capable only of resisting fragmentation and pistol bullets. Russia, 1942. © Bundesarchiv

50 ARMS AND ARMOUR OF THE SECOND WORLD WAR

THE ASSAULT

The crucial final phase of any firefight was when the attacking soldiers, having achieved fire superiority (whether with a machine gun, rifle fire, support weapons or a combination), moved in to take the ground they had been fighting for. Each of the combatant nations took a different approach to the assault phase. In 1939 the weapon best suited to the assault was the submachine gun, a fact that Britain was slow to appreciate. Being compact, with high-capacity magazines and much less recoil from their pistol ammunition, these were designed for rapid or automatic fire. This prevented the enemy from firing back on the approach, increased hit probability and increased close-range lethality.

With its low-power pistol ammunition, the submachine gun was of limited use beyond 100m. The US squad at least had the M1 Garand, enabling every rifleman to fire all eight rounds in his magazine as fast as he could pull the trigger. Every other nation was reliant upon bolt-action rifles. The British Enfields had the advantage of ten-round magazines, provided the rifleman had time to 'top off' his magazine prior to the assault phase of the firefight. Bolt-actions could be cycled and fired more rapidly from the hip (especially if the bolt was cycled with index finger and thumb, and the middle finger pulled the trigger). This was extremely inaccurate, however, and without the ability to fire multiple shots quickly, the chances of hitting the target were greatly reduced. As a result, these nations were obliged to place significant reliance upon the 'shock effect' of the bayonet (see p. 71) in the assault. This was somewhat mitigated by judicious use of the squad's machine gun and the squad leader's personal weapon (even if at first, for the British Empire, this was only a pistol), but what was needed was an automatic weapon firing rifle-type ammunition that one man could easily operate. Such weapons had been available since 1915 with the French CSRG 'Chauchat' and 1918 with the US Browning Automatic Rifle but they remained cumbersome.

▲ When firing at a distance soldiers were taught to fire single shots from the shoulder. This was more accurate as the gun was stable and the soldier could line up the sights.

HANDLING AND SIGHTING

FIRING FROM THE SHOULDER. —The left hand must grip the gun. On the Mk. III gun there is a projection against which the little finger may rest. The right hand holds the butt and operates the trigger, which is a single pull-off. The gun must be firmly held and pressed well into the shoulder.

FIRING FROM THE HIP. Keep the left hand and wrist clear of the magazine, holding the gun with the hand clear of the ejection opening. Hold the gun firmly into the hip and point the muzzle at the target. Fire short bursts, observing the fire. "Double taps"—that is, firing of two shots when set for single shots —indicates loose holding. Cultivate a determined attitude well balanced with left foot forward and knee bent.

▲ This page from the period manual 'The Sten Machine Carbine' shows the two main methods of firing. The 'hip', 'waist' or (literally) the 'assault' position allowed for full control of the muzzle in automatic mode and was commonly used until the 1990s.

Only one nation pursued the possibility of a new type of weapon, one that would give every rifleman the capability to turn his self-loading rifle into a submachine gun at the flick of a switch. That nation was Nazi Germany and that weapon was the assault rifle: today's standard-issue infantry weapon worldwide.

PPSH-41 7.62 MM SUBMACHINE GUN

Like Germany, the Soviet Union had recognised the importance of rapidity and volume of fire before the war, introducing the PPD-34 in 1935. Unlike the other combatant nations, it decided to move beyond the typical limited issue of submachine guns. At Stalingrad (1942) the 'storm group' concept was introduced, similar to German doctrine in that the attacking groups were backed by a support group with heavy machine guns, anti-tank rifles and mortars, but with the attacking men armed with submachine guns in lieu of rifles. By 1943 up to half of the infantry platoon were to be so equipped. This increased issue inevitably increased tactical emphasis on closing with the enemy, since the short-barrelled pistol-calibre arms could not be effectively used beyond 200 metres.

Up to that range, though, the PPSh excelled. Since the Red Army utilised the company as their primary tactical unit, typically there would be men armed with longer-ranged weapons at hand where needed. In line with this doctrine, the 71-round drum magazine allowed the PPD-34, PPD-40 and (in 1942) the improved PPSh-41 to maintain bursts of fire for much longer than other weapons before reloading. Due to production limitations these drums were not interchangeable, although the two drums issued with each gun gave similar capacity (142 rounds) to multiple box magazines or around 30 rounds in other systems. Rate of fire was several hundred rounds per minute higher, however, at around 900 rounds per minute. Despite this a relatively effective compensator, formed as part of the stamped steel receiver/heatshield, directed firing gas upward and helped to counter muzzle rise. The PPSh – or 'PapaSha' as it was pronounced – was supplemented by the even cheaper PPS-43 but remained in production and use until war's end.

◀ A 1944-dated example of the PPSh-41. PR.11629

▲ These Russian soldiers are fighting Germans with PPSh-41 submachine guns. The PPSh was well-suited to these urban battles but fired weak ammunition. Stalingrad, November 1942. © Wikicommons/Sovfoto

M1 'GARAND' SELF-LOADING RIFLE

In 1936 the United States of America became the first nation to adopt a self-loading rifle (a rifle firing one shot each time the trigger is pulled) for regular military service. The ability to fire rapidly gave a significant advantage in combat and made it easier to train soldiers to shoot well. They could keep the rifle aimed at the target instead of having to operate a bolt or a lever to eject the fired cartridge case and load a fresh round into the rifle's chamber. America's new rifle was designed by Canadian John Cantius Garand. It held eight rounds of .30 calibre (.30-06) ammunition, loaded into 'en bloc' clips that were inserted into the rifle and automatically ejected when empty. The mechanism used a version of the gas piston system first patented by Sir Hiram Maxim in 1883.

▲ M1 'Garand' self-loading rifle, 1942. PR.13333

▲ Clip of .30-06 ammunition (front).

▲ Clip of .30-06 ammunition (side).

▲ Bolt locked open ready to receive a clip.

THE ASSAULT 55

▲ An American soldier armed with the standard issue M1 rifle. Kentucky, USA, 1942.
© Alfred T. Palmer/US Library of Congress

US doctrine around firepower is summarised by a January 1943 US War Department publication ('The German Squad in Combat') which reminded readers that 'victory comes to the one who fires the largest number of well-aimed shots against his opponent in the shortest time'. The same source noted that 'German squad tactics differ from those of the US mainly in being based around employment of the squad LMG' and pointed out that the US squad was reliant upon the fire support of external machine-gun units armed with the M1919 Browning. The squad-level M1918A2 BAR with its significant weight and limited 20-round magazine was a poor light machine gun, and it was the M1 rifle that supplied most of the US squad 'base of fire' out to 400 yards.

As Britain soldiered on with its old but faithful Lee rifle, the M1 became a benchmark for military rifles. After the war, some nations followed the German model of the compact, low-recoil, fully automatic 'assault rifle' as the next logical step. The US, however, remained wedded

▲ German soldiers armed with *Sturmgewehr* rifles fighting Americans equipped with M1 Garand rifles in the Ardennes (Luxembourg), December 1944. © Bundesarchiv

to the full-power self-loading rifle until 1963 when it adopted the M16 rifle. Wartime experience with the Garand and its availability to civilians after the war made it an iconic American weapon. Famously, General George S. Patton described the M1 as 'the greatest battle implement ever devised'. There is no doubt that it was superbly effective.

Sergeant William Carr, 116th Infantry Regiment, 29th Infantry Division in Brittany, August 1944 reportedly shot 15 German paratroopers with as many rounds, no doubt due to the Garand's combination of accuracy, terminal effect, and rapidity of fire.

M1 CARBINE

US Army officers and support troops received the lighter and more compact M1 Carbine, also semi-automatic but chambered for the .30 Carbine round. This was effectively a pistol-type cartridge, making the Carbine akin in terms of capacity and effective range to the Thompson submachine gun. It was far lighter than the celebrated Thompson, but lacked the 'punch' of the .45 ACP round and could not fire automatically, leaving an important role for the sub-machine gun. The Carbine's role was different, serving for most users as a more capable replacement for the M1911 pistol. Some infantry soldiers also favoured the lightweight and fast-handling Carbine over other available weapons for patrols. A folding stock variant (the M1A1) was also created for paratroopers. Postwar, the automatic M2 and M3 with infrared night-sight were developed.

▲ A late-war M1 Carbine with improved adjustable rear sight and bayonet lug, added in 1945 after complaints from soldiers. This example saw service with the Royal Hong Kong Police post-war. PR.8691

TOKAREV SVT-40 SELF-LOADING RIFLE

After something of a false start with the AVS-36 and SVT-38 designs, the Soviet Union introduced the SVT-40 in 1940. The designer was Fedor Vasilyevich Tokarev, known for his TT-30 series of self-loading pistols and a senior official in the post-war Soviet government. His rifle was intended to replace the hundreds of thousands of bolt-action Mosin M91/30 rifles then in service, and fired the same 7.62 mm rimmed cartridge. As a semi-automatic weapon capable of a much higher effective rate of fire, its magazine capacity was twice that of the Mosin (ten rather than five). The Soviet Union could not manufacture anywhere near enough SVT-40s to equip all of its soldiers, and so it saw limited service. It was often provided to snipers, who had the additional training to make full use of its capabilities and could keep it in working order (self-loading rifles being less reliable). Self-loading rifles allow the shooter to quickly and accurately follow up their first shot, which was especially important for snipers at this time. Captured examples of the SVT were used by German troops and directly inspired the German G43 rifle. Notably, it was used by Ukrainian-born sniper Ludmila Pavlichenko, who was quoted as saying, 'Every German who remains alive will kill women, children and old folks. Dead Germans are harmless. Therefore, if I kill a German, I am saving lives.' It does appear, however, that Pavlichenko's association with the SVT was driven by Soviet propaganda rather than a clear personal preference.

▲ Sniper Ludmila Pavlichenko, who was specially presented with an SVT rifle by a Soviet general. Pavlichenko was one of around 2500 female snipers active during the war. *Smena Magazine*, No.12, 1942.

ARISAKA TYPE 99 RIFLE

Although most countries involved in the war were obliged to make use of the bayonet in the assault, the Japanese Empire entered the war with substantial reliance upon edged weapons. Japan apparently saw no advantage in self-loading or automatic rifles until it encountered US troops equipped *en masse* with the M1 rifle, which prompted development of the similar Type 4. Emerging for trials only in 1944, it was nowhere near ready for issue at war's end, leaving Japanese infantry largely equipped with bolt-action rifles. The Type 99 was an improved version of the (formerly 6.5×50 mm) Arisaka pattern, chambering the more powerful 7.7 mm (7.7×58 mm) cartridge and was, once again, shorter than earlier variants. Its bayonet remained the 1897-vintage Type 30 pattern, and this was regarded as invaluable in the attack. Although the stereotypical 'banzaii' frontal assault was actually frowned upon in terms of doctrine, a traditional belief in the warrior spirit (parallel to the Western 'spirit of the pike' and especially French reliance upon the bayonet in the First World War) saw these assaults launched regularly. Japanese (and indeed Russian) doctrine called for bayonets to be fixed at all times, in contrast to Western armies where they were fitted only prior to a final assault or if advancing through urban or trench environments. Japan was also the only country to issue swords to infantry, in the form of the *shin guntō* sword, a mass-produced take on the traditional Samurai *katana* that was issued to non-commissioned officers. Commissioned officers, like those of Western nations, carried swords for ceremonial purposes, often antique *katana* in contemporary mounts.

▲ An early Edo-period *katana* remounted for Second World War service and said to have belonged to a General Murai. XXVIS.341

▲ Surrendered Japanese forces give up their swords to the British 25th Indian Division in Malaya (now Malaysia), 1945. © IWM IND 4851

▲ The Japanese Type 99 rifle. PR.638

TYPE 96 LIGHT MACHINE GUN

All of this may give the impression of a military stuck in the past, but in fact Japan's squad light machine gun was close to the modern concept of the 'assault machine gun', designed to be light, short, and portable. It is the only issue machine gun ever designed to mount a bayonet – the same Type 30 as the infantry rifle. Despite this odd anachronism, the Type 96 was very much a modern squad automatic. Although quite different to the

THE ASSAULT 61

▲ The Type 30 bayonet was used on both Type 99 rifle and Type 96 machine gun. X.337

British Bren, its superficial resemblance speaks to its advanced design and (bayonettings notwithstanding) modern tactical employment. Japanese squads were not called 'rifle sections' but 'light machine gun sections' and platoon tactics favoured enveloping attacks in which two squads would fix the enemy whilst the third flanked and pressed the assault.

◀ The Type 96 light machine gun, with bayonet lug and spigot visible below the barrel. PR.13348

ROAD TO THE 'ASSAULT RIFLE'

The German armed forces ended up with not one but three different solutions to the assault problem. Firstly, correctly identifying the potential of the M1 and SVT-40, it initiated development of its own equivalent. The famous firms of Mauser and Walther were commissioned to come up with prototypes. Only Mauser followed the military requirement to the letter, providing a bolt-action style cocking handle for emergency manual operation. Walther's rival G41(W) design ignored this aspect and as a result was commissioned to develop what was dubbed the *Gewehr* 43, later shortened and redesignated the *Karabiner* 43. Technically it compared favourably with its foreign rivals, offering a similar size (shorter than the SVT), weight, capacity (two more than the Garand), accuracy and reliability. Although featuring a 10-round detachable magazine, this could also be reloaded from the top using five-round Kar98K stripper clips in an emergency (saving the time necessary to remove the magazine and load individual rounds into it).

FG42 PARATROOPER RIFLE

For a time it looked as though the G43 would be a straightforward like-for-like replacement for the Kar98K, just as the Garand had entirely replaced the Springfield M1903 in US Army (if not US Marine) service. The first design to throw a spanner in the works was the *Fallschirmjagergewehr* 42 (FG 42), designed at the behest of the *Luftwaffe* for their paratroopers. Following a disaster on Crete in 1941 in which German paratroopers were unable to quickly access their rifles and machine guns. The heavy casualties sustained were blamed in part upon this deficiency, and so work began on a 'jack-of-all-trades' weapon that could be carried on the body in a parachute drop, providing some of the capability of a rifle, submachine gun and light machine gun rolled into one. Louis Stange of Rheinmetall-Borsig took design lead.

The result was a relatively light automatic rifle derived from the Lewis gun. It chambered the standard 7.92 mm rifle/machine gun cartridge and its handguard folded down to act as a bipod, allowing it to act much like the

▲ The Walther-designed G43 rifle. This example was made at their Zella-Mehlis factory in Thuringia, in 1944. PR.6659

▲ The original pattern of FG 42 rifle with distinctive slanted pistol grip, designed to prevent snagging on equipment. PR.6669

British Bren gun when fired in bursts and was similarly accurate in semi-automatic mode and controllable in automatic fire (due to a highly effective muzzle brake). Unlike the Bren it was short and light. It could certainly replace the Kar98K and even the new G43, and even sported a spike bayonet, stowed reversed under the handguards. It could even serve as a sniper rifle via an

THE ASSAULT 65

▲ The first pattern FG42 featured a folding bipod and reversible bayonet under the barrel. PR.6669

optional ZfG 42 4-power magnification sight. Although heavier and bulkier than a submachine gun, it was very compact and could stand in for one if needed. Its internal gas piston and barrel were made as short as possible. The magazine was sited on the side of the weapon. Even the sights were made to fold for carriage. Overall the FG 42 achieved what it was supposed to, but like so many other wartime designs, there were insufficient resources to produce enough. Less than 10,000 were manufactured by war's end.

STURMGEWEHR 44 (STG 44)

The ultimate Nazi firearm for the assault, both in terms of design success and in chronological terms, was the *Sturmgewehr* 44 (StG 44), inextricably married to its special 7.9 mm Kurz (7.92×33 mm) ammunition. This was the final name for a series of weapons that began with the *Maschinenkarabiner 42* (Haenel-designed) or 'MKb 42(H)'. Easily distinguished by the full-length gas tube/piston housing above the barrel, this was issued to troops for field trials in early summer 1943. Captured examples informed the development of the iconic Kalashnikov design of 1947. From 1943 to 1944 it was developed as the MP 43/1, MP 43, MP 44 and StG 44. The last three of these were identical, bearing different designations for political reasons.

Hitler took some persuading that this unproven concept should be put into the field as a rifle, and was prepared at first only to regard it as an improved submachine gun (*Maschinenpistole* or MP). Eventually he agreed and is said to have personally

▲ An MP43/1, the first production variant of the *Sturmgewehr*. PR.5357

▲ The *Sturmgewehr* was a truly modern 'assault rifle' and was even trialled with an optical sight, a standard feature of today's infantry rifles. © Bundesarchiv

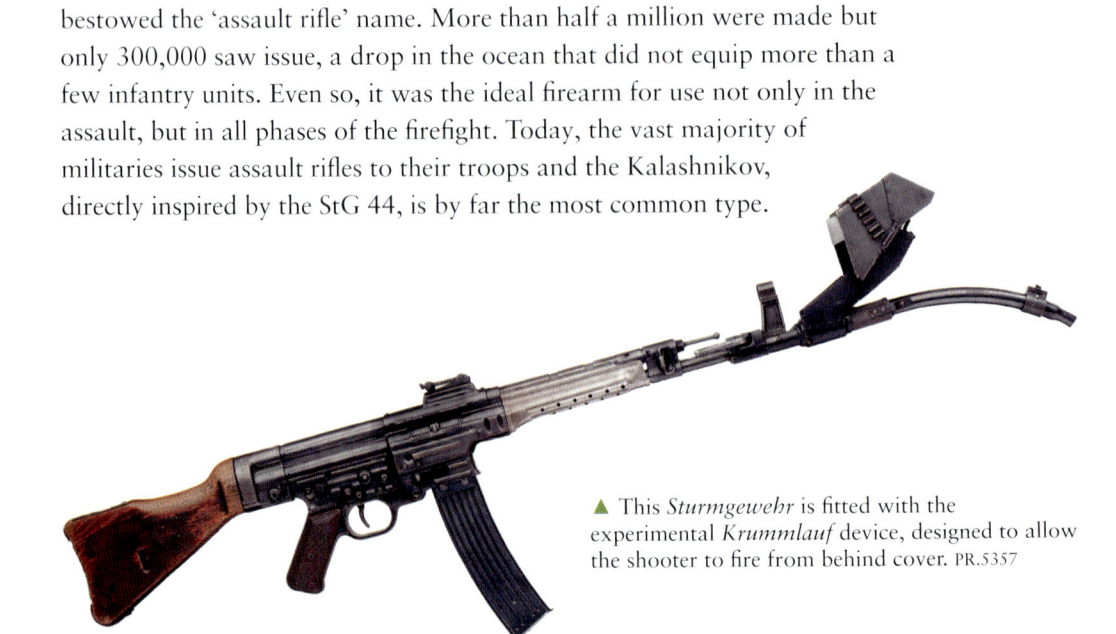

bestowed the 'assault rifle' name. More than half a million were made but only 300,000 saw issue, a drop in the ocean that did not equip more than a few infantry units. Even so, it was the ideal firearm for use not only in the assault, but in all phases of the firefight. Today, the vast majority of militaries issue assault rifles to their troops and the Kalashnikov, directly inspired by the StG 44, is by far the most common type.

▲ This *Sturmgewehr* is fitted with the experimental *Krummlauf* device, designed to allow the shooter to fire from behind cover. PR.5357

68 ARMS AND ARMOUR OF THE SECOND WORLD WAR

TRAINING TO KILL

The First World War had seen increasing dehumanisation of the German enemy as the unfeeling murderous 'Boche' or 'Hun', particularly after attacks on civilians. Thomas Nash, private in the Manchester Regiment on the Western Front remarked of trench fighting that '"kill, kill, kill" was the motto'. This harsh reality was not, however, reflected in official doctrine and training, which took its moral lead from late-19th century developments in international law. Agreements like the St Petersburg and Hague conventions were enacted in response to new, more deadly weapons like the repeating rifle, machine gun, and quick-firing artillery. These threatened to destroy the remnants of 'gentlemanly' warfare of earlier periods. It is arguable whether such attitudes ever truly existed, but officers at least were taught the theory – that one fought to incapacitate the enemy, not to necessarily kill him.

Training materials lacked any mention of killing, nor did they spell out the purpose of issued weapons. Even with the bayonet, soldiers were taught to thrust into sandbags, albeit with a greater degree of aggression than when engaging targets with firearms or throwing grenades. International law, which only covered war between signatory nation states, reaffirmed this intention and sought to impose limits upon the types of weapons and ammunition used in warfare. Despite fanning the flames of anti-German sentiment, the British government had nonetheless sought the moral high ground, avoiding overt bloodlust and even refraining from bombing German civilians until summer 1918 despite Zeppelin attacks on the British population as early as 1915. Neither international law nor moral restraint was able to prevent the development of weapons like flamethrowers and poison gas in the First World War, nor to make a dent in the horrific death toll of that conflict.

Without the stalemate trench fighting of the Great War, the Second World War did not see the same use of chemical weapons, but weapons of all kinds (including incendiary types) continued to develop and proliferate. Far from reigning in the excesses of the previous war, renewed German aggression led to a sense that an old enemy with no scruples of his own had reemerged. This caused Britain in particular (but not uniquely) to abandon any prior pretence of chivalry. New weapons, new training, new types of units to operate behind enemy lines, and new attitudes systemically weaponised anti-German sentiment. This was well summarised by Lt. E. Hartley Leather in his book *Combat Without Weapons* (1942):

All Germans live for just one purpose and that is exterminating all Englishmen; and therefore the only hope of winning this war is in our doing the job first.

The existing series of Small Arms Training pamphlets were revised in 1942 to incorporate new weapons but also this new philosophical approach. Into each manual was inserted the following line to make the deadly job of the weapon clear to the trainer and therefore to the recruit:

The sole object of weapon training is to teach all ranks the most efficient way of handling their weapons in order to kill the enemy.

▶ This image of Prime Minister Winston Churchill was used in a Nazi propaganda leaflet playing on long-standing British reservations against 'gangster' weapons like the Thompson. Instead it reinforced the intent of the original photograph – that Britain would fight back by any means necessary.
© IWM H 2646A

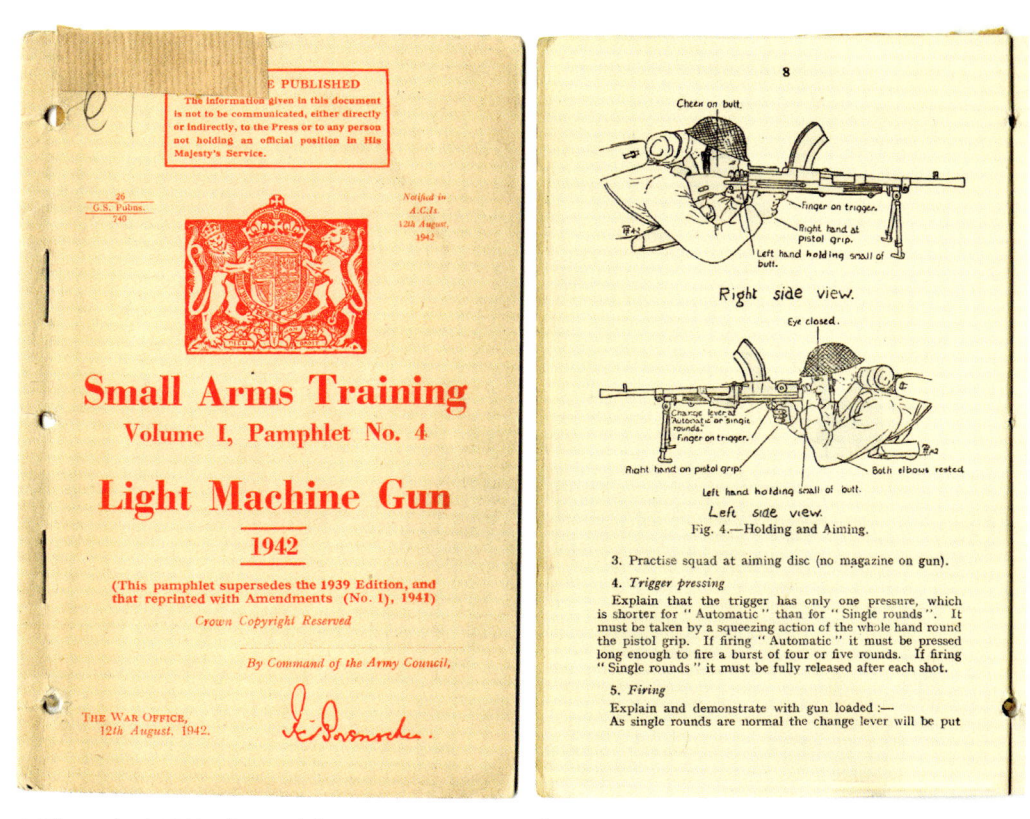

▲ The revised 1942 edition of the Bren training manual. RAL.27398

For the bayonet, additional emphasis was added with the phrases 'Instructors will always bear this in mind and will continually impress it upon those whom they instruct', and 'The object of bayonet training is, firstly, to make the man confident in his ability to kill with the bayonet and secondly, by means of collective exercises, to train the section or platoon to work together as a team'. Here the emphasis is reversed over the prior (1937) edition of the same manual. In addition, for the first time (in writing at least), instructors were told to get the men shouting at the enemy 'to raise their own morale and to intimidate the enemy'. At the same time, however, mention of silent assaults in which soldiers were to advance with their cold steel as silently as possible whilst making use of hand signals was also included. In this way both raw aggression and stealthy surprise killing were both prepared for.

In practical terms the training programme was reduced from six lessons to four, and the practice of 'hip-firing' was introduced. It advised that 'during and advance and when about 10 yds from the enemy, it may be advisable to fire a bullet' and that riflemen should 'instantly reload, and return "on guard"'. This practice can be seen in period training films such as 'Platoon in the Attack', preserved in the collections of the Imperial War Museum and Australian War Memorial.

This new explicit recognition of the true purpose of weapons was also reinforced in the official training film 'Use of Fire', the narration of which exclaimed that 'the first and most important use of fire in battle (is) to kill', at which point the words 'TO KILL' filled the screen to underscore the point. To further push home the point, it then pointed out that this was 'obvious, but very important'. This admitted statement of the obvious speaks to the altered collective British mindset. Military language was no longer polite, abstract or euphemistic. It was now overt, even bloodthirsty. This extended from front-line specialist troops like the Commandos to members of the Home Guard. Of course, the job of the soldier had not actually changed. Although the authorities may have feared a peacetime generation gone soft since the horrors of the last war, many were all too aware of the brutal nature of their job even without such exhortations. Some were resigned to it, others relished it. Lieutenant Neil McCallum, 5/7th Gordon Highlanders remarked in his memoir:

The aim of this uniformed, cohesive and disciplined super-organisation is, of course, to murder. To beat the enemy one must kill him in large numbers … The soldier fights coldly, scientifically, with weapons that kill, for an object that can never be defined so exactly that it satisfies the intellect.

Stanley Whitehouse struggled with the fetishisation of arms that this situation fostered, directly referencing the 'sole purpose' that the War Department chose to leverage in its new training programme:

As I turned away I spotted a fine-looking automatic rifle [an FG 42] on the ground. Picking it up to admire it, I noticed it was in immaculate condition, with the bolt area still greased. Then, inexplicably, a kind of strange nausea swept over me. Why was I admiring this weapon, whose sole purpose was to kill people? I was sick of killing people. Barely able to stop myself from vomiting, I smashed the gun against the wall several times and threw it into the nearby undergrowth.

By contrast, author George MacDonald Fraser in *Quartered Safe Out Here: A Recollection of the War in Burma* (2000) admitted that he and his comrades fully subscribed to government and media propaganda:

It may appal a generation who have been dragooned into considering racism the ultimate crime, but I believe there was a feeling (there was in me) that the Jap was farther down the human scale than the European [...] No doubt newspaper reports and broadcasts had encouraged us, civilians and military, to regard him as an evil, misshapen, buck-toothed barbarian who looked and behaved like something sub-Stone Age; the experiences of Allied prisoners of war demonstrated that the reports had not lied and reinforced the view that the only good Jap was a dead one. And we were right, then.

COMBAT WITHOUT WEAPONS

INTRODUCTION

THIS little book is written with just two objects in view—brevity and simplicity. There are numerous texts on the subject, which is really a simplified version of the well-known jiu-jitsu. Unfortunately, most people still find it rather complicated and involved, and in this short volume we will try to reduce it to its lowest common denominator. Our idea is not to attempt to make specialists out of average people, but simply to teach a few simple tricks that everyone can learn in a matter of minutes, that will make you more efficient at the task we all have to hand—exterminating Germans.

The phrase "exterminating Germans" is used purposely, because we must always remember that *all* Germans live for just one purpose, and that is exterminating *all* Englishmen; and therefore the only hope of winning this war is in our doing the job first. Every honest man must believe that to-day, and if he does not believe it he is not an honest man.

No matter how unsavoury the job may be, it has got to be done, and done thoroughly; remember, the German is always thorough: we will only beat him if we play his own game, because he will never play ours. Sportsmanship and decency are entirely foreign to his nature. Kicking a man when he is down does not appeal to the average Briton, but we must forget our long-learned niceties when dealing with the Boche; the Nazi is congenitally incapable of being decent. It is not a matter solely of beating the Hun; it is even more than that—a matter of saving your own life and those of your wife and your children.

◀ The unofficial manual *Combat Without Weapons* (1942) taught that their primary goal was 'exterminating Germans'. RAL.23192

FIG. 2.—THE WITHDRAWAL FROM THE POINT

▲ 'Withdrawal from the Point', from *Small Arms Training Vol 1 Pamphlet 12* (1942).

The British authorities decided to start actively teaching soldiers to see the enemy as sub-human, to despise them and to try to kill them outright, regardless of international convention. Special 'Hate Training' sessions were organised in which recruits were shown photographs of German atrocities, animal blood was added to bayonet training, and tours were arranged of local abattoirs to not only direct anger and violence toward Germans but to acclimatise themselves to blood, death and killing. 'Hate Training' was deemed neither sufficiently realistic nor an efficient way to increase aggression and was dropped in May 1942.

◀ The British No.69 grenade was introduced in 1940 as an offensive purpose grenade that created a stunning blast without dangerous fragments. It was found to be ineffective and was repurposed for realistic training purposes. XX.4976

Far more successful was the drive (shared with most militaries) simply to make training more realistic, aiming to embed skills and reactions that soldiers would carry directly over to real combat without thinking. Known in Britain as 'battle drills', these were intended as jumping-off points for actual tactics. Officers and NCOs were taught to think for themselves and adapt the basic drills to the situation at hand rather than merely enacting them by the book. Soldiers not only fired at human-shaped but moving targets, and conducted large-scale realistic field exercises. The Commandos took this a step further with real explosives and live ammunition in proximity to recruits. This style of training (albeit made less dangerous!) remains in use across the world today, and although 'hate training' is long gone, the basic shift in attitude from teaching incapacitation to instilling the drive to kill arguably remains.

▲ A British infantry platoon practises an amphibious landing as explosive charges are detonated close by. BEN 134

FLAMETHROWERS

Perhaps the most controversial of pre-war weapons was the flamethrower, which projected a stream of thickened, burning fuel and created horrific injuries as well as burning away oxygen and introducing choking fumes into the immediate area. This was especially effective in enclosed spaces like trenches, and reinforced structures like pillboxes. They could also be used to destroy abandoned civilian buildings occupied by enemy forces. Britain had complained about German flamethrowers in the First World War but now sought to literally fight fire with fire by developing its own compact portable version. The resulting No.2 Mk.II 'Lifebuoy' backpack flamethrower with its distinctive circular fuel tank had a range of around 50 yards and were initially supplied to airborne and Commando units and the Canadian infantry.

▲ A German flamethrower being used to destroy a house. Eastern Europe, *c.*1943. © IWM COL 000176

▲ The first British flamethrower, nicknamed 'Lifebuoy' because of its round backpack tanks. © IWM H 37975

▶ No. 5 Mk.1 'Ack Pack' flame gun without its backpack fuel tank. PR.7448

TRAINING TO KILL 77

'Lifebuoy' was first used in combat in Normandy in August 1944. *The Times* reported using language that again reflects the overt shift in British attitudes to killing and 'terror', justified by the resulting Commonwealth lives saved:

After literally burning and blasting their way through Hitler's Atlantic Wall [these weapons] have since saved the lives of countless attacking British and Canadian infantry in Normandy by subduing and terrorising the enemy in his strong-points with gun and flame. That was the specific purpose for which they were created.

'GANGSTER' GUNS

The British Army had encountered German submachine guns in the First World War but was slow to recognise their value. Because of criminal use between the wars, they were regarded as uncivilised weapons or 'gangster guns'. The outbreak of war came as a 'reality check' for the British authorities and an initial 750 American Thompson guns were purchased in 1940, numbers totalling 108,000 by 1941. The Thompson design was too slow to manufacture in sufficient quantities specifically for the UK, however, and so further procurement was carried out under the Lend-Lease scheme.

British contract Thompsons were the Model 1928, with the Lyman adjustable backsight and, for the most part, the Cutts compensator and front pistol grip. Oddly, they were provided with only a single sling loop, being on the buttstock underside, leaving British armourers the task of affixing a forward loop. These Model 1928 guns maintained the questionable Blish lock system, which operated on the assumption that interaction of different types of metals produces greater friction than like metals, and so were fitted with a brass 'H'-shaped locking piece. Thompsons provided to Britain under the Lend-Lease scheme were marked as the Model 1928A1, and had US acceptance and property markings.

By war's end 651,086 M1928 model Thompsons had been provided to the UK via purchase and (mainly) Lend-Lease, representing around 15% of British service submachine guns. Most saw service with the Commando brigades and the Home Guard, although section commanders in the regular infantry also carried them until the far more cost-effective Sten gun became available in quantity. It was extremely heavy, weighing almost three pounds more than the Mk.II Sten, but tended to be more reliable and was well-liked. British service examples are identical to US ones save for inspection marks on early guns and modification to the sling swivels. British guns lacked the distinctive front pistol grip (to this day the vertical foregrip on the L85 service rifle is known colloquially as the 'gangster grip').

The view of the Thompson as a gangster weapon was seemingly institutionalised, whether individuals held a positive, rakish view of it or a negative one. George MacDonald Fraser remarked after the war that 'for some reason I felt like a bully, just carrying it'. Fraser, who appreciated the precision and build quality of the Lee-Enfield rifle, eventually threw his assigned Thompson away in favour of an SMLE captured from a soldier of the Indian National Army (enemies of the British Raj). Most British soldiers coveted the image and firepower of the submachine gun, however. Corporal Alex Bowlby, who had turned down command of a section, actively sought (and was provided with from stores) a Thompson to replace his rifle. Even when issued the British machine carbine, the comparisons were there, as Lance Corporal Rex M. Wingfield, 1/6th Queen's Regiment, noted: 'At the end of the column was Burt, his Sten at the hip, moving backwards like an American gangster leaving a bank'.

Considering the Thompson gun's thoroughly American origins and its ubiquity in popular culture, the US Army did not, ironically, issue them to its infantry squads or even platoons. Per the official Table of Equipment, just six Thompsons were provided at company level, to be issued on a mission-specific basis. In practice though, individual soldiers would acquire them however they could. The Thompson saw more extensive service in the US Marine Corps, notably in the hands of squad commanders.

▲ A British contract Auto-Ordnance Thompson M1928A1. PR.1334

▲ British soldiers with the Thompson M1928A1 submachine gun from *Picture Post*, 20 July 1940. The associated article highlighted the weapon's use by US law enforcement to soften the stigma of the 'gangster gun'.

SNIPING EVOLVES

By 1918 most had recognised the value of the telescopic sight in shooting individual enemy combatants at distance. Each nation adopted specialised variants of its standard issue infantry rifle, selected from the production line for inherent accuracy and fitted with telescopic sights and mounts. Having failed to introduce an effective rifle and scope combination in the First World War, Britain was again slow to adopt one. The No.4 Mk.I (T) sniper variant of the Lee-Enfield did not see issue until 1942.

Arguably the most iconic sniper rifle of the war was the Russian Mosin rifle, better known in the West as the 'Mosin-Nagant'. Used by Soviet snipers alongside the standard M91/30 infantry rifle, the Mosin sniper was fitted with PU and later PE pattern telescopic sights, both with slightly greater 3.5x magnification than the 3x British No.32. It was not only used to great effect by Soviet snipers but also those on the Finnish side in the 1939–40 'Winter War' like Simo Häyhä. Häyhä carried the Finnish-made M/28-30 copy of the Mosin and the Finnish Suomi KP/-31 submachine gun. Unusually, he used both weapons to actively hunt and kill the enemy, seemingly with equal success. Typically, snipers who carried a submachine gun did so as a personal defence weapon, pistols being more common for this purpose for reasons of mobility.

▲ The Mosin Pattern 1891/30 7.62 mm bolt-action rifle with PU telescopic sight. PR.6476

The further away the sniper could be, the safer he would be and the more damage he could inflict before discovery and/or return fire. This distance, along with the cold, calculated attitude needed to stalk and hunt men unable to defend themselves, led to a negative reaction not only from enemy soldiers (who would hurt or kill captured snipers) but even from their comrades. Rex Wingfield related:

We didn't like snipers. Ordinary infantry were doing a job, like us, but snipers were low, nasty, mean fighters [...] In their own way they were doing their job, but it was a dirty job.

The emotionless approach that the ordinary soldier so distrusted was seen by some as essential to effective sniping. Captain C. Shore pointed out that the sort of attitude actively being instilled in most soldiers (see Chapter 5) was actually counter-productive:

I often heard it said that a sniper should be a man filled with a deadly hatred of the Hun, or enemy. But I found that the men who had seething hatred in their hearts for all things German, such as those who had lost their wives and children and homes in the blitzed cities, were not the type to make good rifle killers. The type I wanted was the man of cold precision, the peace-time hunter who had no hatred for his quarry but just a great interest in the stalk and the kill.

BOYS .55 IN ANTI-TANK RIFLE

The monstrous bolt-action Boys rifle was introduced in 1937 as the platoon's tank-killer. Able to penetrate only 23.2 mm (0.91 in) of armour at 100 yards (91 m) it was unable to knock out the new German Panzer III and was thus technically obsolescent immediately. It nonetheless saw use in the Far East theatre and with the Commandos, for whom it was particularly useful. The Commandos trained with the Boys at their training centre at Lochailort in Scotland, evidenced by fired cases recovered archaeologically and identified by the author in 2011. Ammunition and realistic targets were both apparently at a premium, however, since author David Lee quotes Private Alan Coote of A Troop, No.4 Commando, as having remarked that his 'only previous experience with this weapon was a few shots on the field firing range'. The intended targets were what is now termed 'materiel' – lightly protected vehicles, structures and critical equipment, foreshadowing the proliferation in the 1980s of the 'anti-materiel rifle' or AMR (exemplified by the famous US Barrett 'Fifty'). Lee refers to a Commando by the name of McDonough putting a flak tower out of action with 'something like sixty rounds from his shoulder with his anti-tank rifle'. Will Fowler, meanwhile, documents in 'Commandos at Dieppe – Rehearsal for D-Day' the use of the Boys to disable German Flak 88 anti-aircraft guns. Like modern AMRs, it could also be used to engage enemy infantry behind cover such as walls or sandbags. Its large and heavy bullet (more than half an inch in diameter and 946 grain, or 61 grams, in weight) would inflict horrific wounds even having passed through cover. The downside was the significant weight of the rifle (35 lb or 16 kg) and high recoil. Even when issued to an ordinary infantry section, only specially trained soldiers would be issued it. The Boys stayed in significant production until September 1943 despite the PIAT being in major production by that point, perhaps due to its repurposing against targets other than tanks. Thus the Boys, while instantly obsolete for its design purpose, was still extremely useful.

◀ The shortened airborne variant of the Boys Anti-Tank rifle. PR.12363

DE LISLE COMMANDO CARBINE

Conceived for Commando service from the outset, the De Lisle was designed by William Godfray De Lisle, an engineer in the Ministry of Aircraft Production. It combined the old Lee-Enfield bolt-action with a specially designed and highly effective silencer ('sound suppressor'). De Lisle began work in 1942 with the intention of making a silenced hunting rifle, but his work proved of great interest to the authorities. By this time the British Commandos had been created with the mission of attacking behind enemy lines using surprise and stealth, creating a need for a silenced rifle for killing sentries and guard dogs. The barrel was taken from the Thompson submachine gun and was drilled with holes to allow the suppressor around it to work more effectively. The suppressor, with its metal baffles and rubber 'wipes', allowed propellant gases to expand and cool, greatly reducing the report. The .45 ACP bullet was already slower than the speed of sound, and with a manual bolt that could be quietly closed, the De Lisle was one of the quietest weapons ever made. Only 600 were manufactured and it is not known how much use these saw during the Second World War. They were however used during the Malayan Emergency of the 1950s by both military personnel and civilians (who used them to defend their land from insurgents).

▲ A production example of the De Lisle Carbine. PR.5737

▲ The De Lisle Carbine stripped showing the complex construction of its suppressor. PR.9138

FAIRBAIRN-SYKES FIGHTING KNIFE

The famous 'F-S knife' is often called a 'dagger', but having been designed as much for cutting as stabbing, it is definitively a 'fighting knife'. It was created by and named for two British-born Shanghai police officers, William Ewart Fairbairn and Eric Anthony Sykes. By the 1930s the Chinese port city of Shanghai was suffering from significant levels of violent crime and desperately needed a well trained and equipped police force. For Fairbairn and Sykes, the solution was to develop a new martial art incorporating hand-to-hand and knife-fighting techniques and to design their own fighting knife to suit it. The new system, called 'Defendu', was based upon Japanese Jujitsu and European boxing. It was published in the instruction book *All-In Fighting* (1942) and taught to British and Allied armed forces during the Second World War.

The knife was produced in three patterns, each becoming simpler and therefore quicker to produce. This is an example of the second pattern, which was usually blackened to avoid catching the light and revealing the user at night. The knives were issued to Special Operations Executive operatives and in large numbers to Commando soldiers, to whom it became an important symbol of elite status. Royal Marine and British Army soldiers who complete the Commando training course today are entitled to wear insignia that features the knife, and some still choose to purchase the knives.

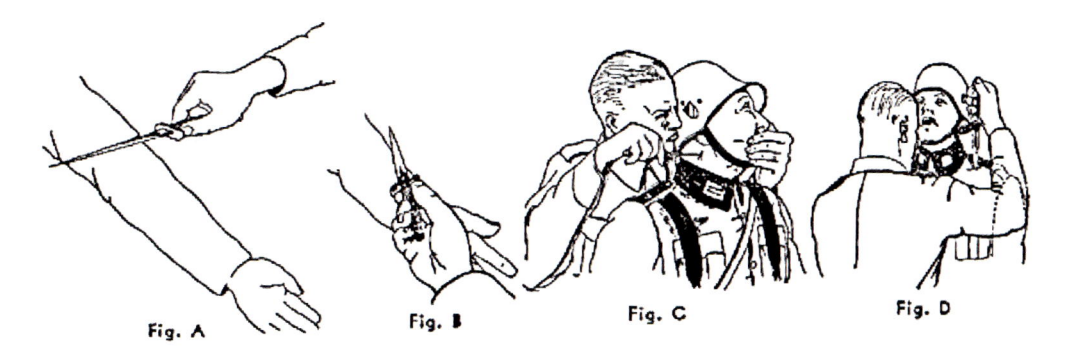

▲ Illustration from *How to win in hand to hand fighting* by Major W.E. Fairburn, showing how the Fairburn-Sykes knife could be used to cut major arteries.

▲ The first pattern F-S knife with distinctive steel hilt, wavy guard and Wilkinson-marked ricasso on the blade. X.732

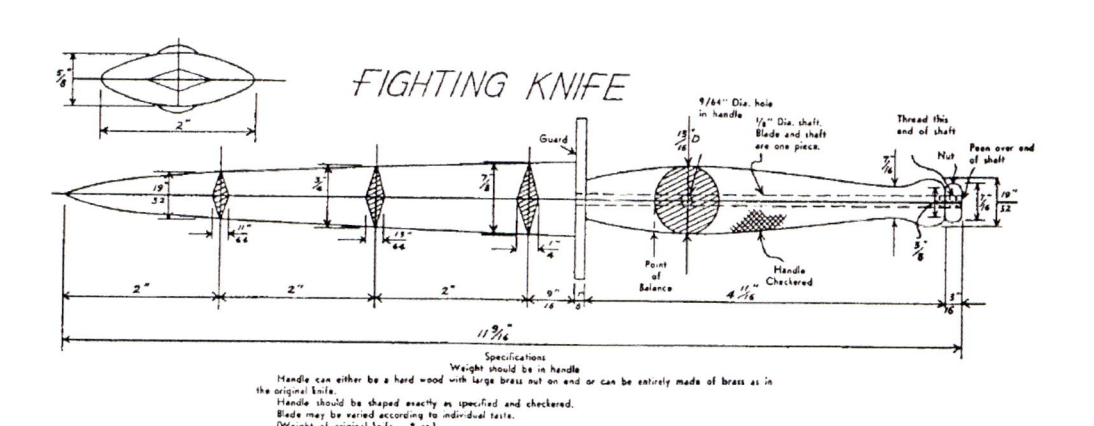

▲ A drawing of the F-S knife from *Kill or Get Killed* (the US equivalent of *All-In Fighting*).

TRAINING TO KILL 85

SILENCED PISTOLS

Special Operations Executive also had a requirement for 'silenced' or sound-suppressed weapons. The unit was formed to operate behind enemy lines and support foreign partisan fighters, and was dubbed 'The Department of Ungentlemanly Warfare' by its first head, Hugh Dalton. The most famous silenced SOE weapon was the Welrod, named, like most SOE gadgets, after Welwyn Garden City in Bedfordshire where it was designed, as well as for its rod-like shape. Three main versions were produced from 1942, initially in .32 ACP (the .32 Mk. I and II) and later the 9 mm Parabellum version seen here (9 mm Mk.I). A derivative for concealment inside a sleeve, the Sleeve Gun, was also produced, lacking the

◀ The ultimate variant of the Welrod was this 9 mm Mk.I. It is easily identified by its trigger guard, since earlier variants lacked this. PR.9023

▶ The .32 in calibre Mk.II (Mk.IIA shown) was the most common Welrod variant. PR.9023

detachable box magazine/pistol grip and with a thumb trigger at the front (not to be confused with the separate 'Welwand' design).

The weapon is designed around its large sound suppressor (or 'silencer'), which features numerous sheet steel 'baffles' to capture and cool propellant gases. This slowly reduces their high pressure and so reduces the sound of firing, just like letting air out of a balloon instead of popping it. Several rubber 'wipes' help to seal around the bullet as it passes through, and the barrel protrudes into the silencer with holes drilled to bleed off gas into the silencer tube more quickly. The result was a report no louder than a vigorous hand-clap. Welrods were used by special operations forces during and after the Second World War, possibly as late as the 1990 Gulf War. They were also air-dropped during the war to partisans for assassination purposes, notably in Denmark.

CONCLUSION

Small arms and even anti-tank weapons were not war-winning or even battle-winning weapons. Official British war statistics showed that 75% of wounds were caused by shells, bombs or mortar rounds. Only 10% were caused by projectiles, a statistic that included anti-tank shells. The conflict culminated with the deployment of the ultimate weapon – the nuclear bomb, about as far from the humble infantry rifle in terms of killing power and strategic impact as it is possible to get. Yet for the individual soldier and for his squad, every wound was potentially life-changing and therefore his personal weapon, whether rifle, submachine gun or even pistol, was critical.

Assessing which weapons were the most important depended upon doctrine and philosophy, but some form of automatic weapon, sometimes more than one (as in the case of the British Bren and Sten) was critical to generating a 'base of fire' sufficient to obtain (and maintain) fire superiority. Only the United States relied upon rifle fire for this purpose at the squad level and attempted to remedy this by attaching a bipod and buttstock to the M1919 to create the awkward A6 variant. Post-war it would combine the German MG42 and FG42 designs to create the squad-level M60.

Regardless of how the squad was equipped, one thing was certain: without fire superiority, no firefight could be won, no advances made, and no battles won. In this way, even if no single squad weapon was strategically significant, getting the right balance of weapons at that basic level was nonetheless critical. Aircraft, armoured vehicles and artillery might be the truly war-winning technologies but without adequate small arms, infantry would be unable to do the crucial job of taking and holding ground.

If the First World War had been the crucible in which new small arms and light weapons technology was forged, the Second World War was the conflict in which it was tempered and honed. There were no major leaps in firearms operating systems, ammunition technology or even materials. Polymers were only gradually finding their way into service weapons, replacing wooden furniture on a limited basis but providing no structural components. What did change were the designs, which became more efficient, reliable and ergonomic – to the point that they could better serve existing tactical niches and occupy new ones. As a result, the US M1 rifle and the German *Sturmgewehr* were both hugely influential after the war, with individual nations adopting similar weapons. Ultimately the 'intermediate calibre' *Sturmgewehr* concept was the most successful, and it dominates military procurement today. However, these rifles are no longer typically used in automatic mode per their original concept (at least in professional militaries). Rapid aimed shots are widely regarded as more effective than automatic fire, which is utilised in professional armed forces only in emergencies (to break 'contact' with the enemy, for example). The light weight and controllability of a modern assault rifle is nonetheless important to the mobility and firepower of the squad.

Despite this, the most significant small-arms legacy of the war was the general-purpose machine gun, pioneered by Germany with the MG-34 and MG-42. Issued at squad level (and thus under the direct control of the squad leader) it has typically provided the base of fire for infantry around the world, alongside increasingly portable anti-armour and anti-structure munitions and under-barrel and standalone grenade launchers. Even nations which have sought to replicate the increased mobility of the light machine gun concept (as deployed by the UK and Japan in the Second World War) have found that belt-fed machine guns firing full-power rifle cartridges after the German fashion remain the better choice for the typical infantry squad.

The other important outcome of the conflict was the realisation of the need for an anti-tank and anti-structure capability that was always available to the squad when needed, as demonstrated by the Panzerfaust (as opposed to the Company-level Bazooka and PIAT). This gradually became standard post-war, from the US 66-mm Light Anti-tank Weapon (LAW) unguided rocket to the British Next-generation Light Anti-tank Weapon (NLAW) guided missile.

Although most of the weapons covered in this book are no longer in active service (with the notable exception of the MG42, in its MG3 guise), their roles and capabilities, together with the tactics underpinning them, are all still in use. The major shifts now concern optics and electronics, as well as constant efforts to minimise weight (the 'soldier burden' in UK parlance) as new features are added. Modern optical sights enable rifles that are broadly similar to those of 1945 to identify and eliminate the enemy at hundreds of metres, day or night. Although these developments began in the 1940s, they were too late to influence infantry combat during the war; once again, Nazi Germany was at the cutting edge, trialling a 4-power infantry optical sight and an infrared night-sight called *Vampir* on the *Sturmgewehr*. These technologies are now standard worldwide alongside the assault rifle and general-purpose machine guns to which they are fitted. Overall, however (at least in comparison with earlier periods), such changes have been relatively modest. To the infantryman of 1945, today's small-unit tactics would be immediately recognisable.

FURTHER READING

Tactical

Bull, S 2004, *World War II Infantry Tactics: Squad and Platoon*, Oxford, Osprey

Moss, M 2020, *The PIAT: Britain's anti-tank weapon of World War II*, London, Osprey

Special Series No. 3, 1942, *German Military Training*, Military Intelligence Service, War Department, 17 September 1942

Special Series No. 9, 1943, *The German Squad in Combat*, Military Intelligence Service, War Department, 25 January 1943

Personal Perspectives

Bowlby, A 2022, *The Recollections of Rifleman Bowlby*, London, Cassell

MacDonald Fraser, G 2000, *Quartered Safe out Here: A Recollection of the War in Burma*, London, Harper Collins

Shore, C 2012, *With British Snipers to the Reich*, London, Frontline Books

Whitehouse, S and G. B. Bennett 1995, *Fear is the Foe: A Footslogger from Normandy to the Rhine*, London, Robert Hale

Fawbert, Eric 2007, *A Rifleman's Diary*, Victoria, Trafford Publishing

Training Videos

Battle Drill: Use of Fire Part 2 (Use of Fire to Kill), IWM film archive DRA 444

Published by Royal Armouries Museum, Armouries Drive, Leeds LS10 1LT, United Kingdom

www.royalarmouries.org

Copyright © 2025 Trustees of the Royal Armouries

All rights reserved. No part of this publication may be reproduced, stored in a retrieval system or transmitted in any form or by any means, electronical, mechanical, photocopying, recording or otherwise without the prior permission of the publisher.

ISBN 978 1 913013 45 5

Royal Armouries Publishing: Martyn Lawrence

Royal Armouries Licensing: Jacob Bishop and Anna Corrall

Designed by Riverside Publishing Solutions Limited, Salisbury, UK

Printed by Xpedient Print

10 9 8 7 6 5 4 3 2 1

The authorised representative for the EEA is Unicorn Publishing Group, Charleston Studio, Meadow Business Centre, Ringmer, Lewes, Sussex BN8 5RW, UK.

A CIP record for this book is available from the British Library

ALSO FROM ROYAL ARMOURIES PUBLISHING

Archduke Franz Ferdinand and the Era of Assassination

Fighting to Kill: the British Infantry Section in the Second World War

*Saving Lives: Sir Arthur Conan Doyle and the
Campaign for Body Armour, 1914–18*

~

Arms and Armour of Henry VIII

Arms and Armour of Late Medieval Europe

Arms and Armour of the First World War

Arms and Armour of the Elizabethan Court

Arms and Armour of the English Civil Wars

Arms and Armour of the Medieval Joust

Arms and Armour of the Renaissance Joust

Chinese Arms and Armour

Indian Arms and Armour

Islamic Arms and Armour

Japanese Arms and Armour

~

Defence of Houses

Defence of Villages and Small Towns

Fire Control

House to House Fighting

Road Blocks

The Art of Prowling